JEWS IN RUSSIA:
The Last Four Centuries

JEWS IN RUSSIA:
THE LAST FOUR CENTURIES

A Documentary History

by

JONATHAN D. PORATH

UNITED SYNAGOGUE COMMISSION
ON JEWISH EDUCATION

Copyright © 1973 by
THE UNITED SYNAGOGUE OF AMERICA

All rights reserved. No part of this book may be reproduced in any form without permission in writing from the publisher except by a reviewer who may quote brief passages in a review to be printed in a magazine or newspaper. Printed in the United States of America.

Library of Congress Catalog Card No. 73-86746
ISBN 0-8381-0220-4

MANUFACTURED IN UNITED STATES OF AMERICA

To Some Very Close Friends—

    Chacham Yitzchak from Tbilisi
    Reb Yona from Moscow
    Reb Nechemyah and Reb Meir from Leningrad
    Shimon and Yitzchak Emmanuelovitch from Odessa
    Reb Eliezer from Sighet
    Reb Aharon from Turetz
    Ya'akov Yitzchakovitch from America

                This Story Belongs To Them.

ACKNOWLEDGMENTS

I would like to thank those individuals whose cooperation, effort, and encouragement have gone into the making of this book. Those include:

Rabbi Efraim Warshaw, formerly Director of the Hebrew High School of Temple Israel, in Great Neck, New York, for first suggesting that I undertake such a project, and for his guidance in expanding and developing the scope of the material;

Students of the 1967-1968 IV class and the 1969-1970 III class of the Hebrew High School of Temple Israel where the course was taught experimentally for the first time, for their suggestions and time;

Rabbi and Mrs. Tzvi H. Porath of Chevy Chase, Maryland, my parents, who continually encouraged me to pursue this project, and who first enabled me to travel to the Jews of the Soviet Union;

Mr. Herman Gross of Great Neck, New York, and the Herman Gross Foundation for providing me with a travel grant to visit the Soviet Union for the High Holidays of 1968, including Simchat Torah in Moscow;

Rabbi Paul Freedman, Director of United Synagogue Youth, for inviting me to serve as a staff leader in the U.S.Y. European Pilgrimages on five occasions;

Professor Mikhail Confino of Tel Aviv University, formerly Chairman of the Department of Russian Studies at the

Hebrew University, and Professor Shmuel Etinger of the Hebrew University, my Israeli professors of Russian and Russian-Jewish studies, for their methodology, interpretation, and inspiration;

Ms. Devorah Joseph, my research assistant, who pursued the difficult task of securing publisher's permissions for the quoted selections; Dr. Pesach Schindler of Jerusalem, Ms. Deborah Gellman of Niagara Falls and London, and Ms. Lisa Levine of New York who all helped in preparing the final text for publication;

Ms. Vivian Stone, my secretary at the Department of Education, United Synagogue of America, for her help in retyping many pages of the manuscript;

Mr. George Levine, Director of the Book Service of the United Synagogue of America, for his considerable publishing skills and professional acumen, and who brought the manuscript through the various production stages with patience and care.

I am indebted particularly to those who read the final draft of the manuscript, and who shared with me their expert comments and critiques;

Mr. Abraham J. Gittelson, Associate Director of the Central Agency for Jewish Education of Greater Miami, for his invaluable educational suggestions and fine and careful eye;

Professor Leon Shapiro, Associate Professor of Russian Jewish History at Rutgers University, for reviewing the draft for historical fact and detail, and for his critical observations and corrections;

Mr. Abraham J. Bayer, former National Coordinator of the American Jewish Conference on Soviet Jewry, and presently Staff Secretary for International Affairs of the National Jewish Community Relations Advisory Council, for his particular attention to the sections of the book dealing with the contemporary condition of Soviet Jewish life, and for his editing the Projects and Activities Appendix.

Mr. Elie Wiesel, author and teacher, for his continued inspiration, advice, and encouragement; and to

Dr. Morton Siegel, Director of the Commission on Jewish Education of the United Synagogue of America, for allowing me to benefit from his fine historical sense, and for making it possible to have this work published through the Commission.

I must hasten to point out that although it would have been impossible for me to produce this work without the aid and advice of those listed above, the responsibility for errors of fact or interpretation is mine.

It is my hope that this documentary history, and the study of the once flourishing and still great Jewish community of the Soviet Union, will, in some small way, contribute to the remaking of our world in the image of the Almighty, and bring salvation and rest to His people, and the entire world.

JONATHAN D. PORATH

New York City
June, 1973
Iyar, 5733

A WORD OF DIRECTION

The area of Russian and Soviet Jewry has been of great concern to the Jews of America for a number of years. Yet, beyond protest literature and personal narratives, little educational material has been produced in an attempt to teach and convey this interest and feeling. A number of major questions come to mind when presenting the area of Soviet Jewry: What is the genesis of the contemporary Jewish community in Russia? What has been its historical past and fate? What is the connection between the Soviet and Tsarist regimes policies towards the Jews? Who speaks for contemporary Soviet Jewry? What is the relation between Soviet Jewry and American Jewry? The answers to these questions and many others are often ambiguous and contradictory. This text has attempted to convey a sense of groping with these serious historical problems. The Introductory Unit, for example, contains both letters from Jews wishing to leave the USSR, and statements by those who publicly defame Zionism and Israel. The student has to weigh and balance these conflicting positions for himself.

As distinct from a reference text, this collection is designed to examine selectively different aspects of the life of the Russian and Soviet Jewish communities. In general, not more than one document or series of documents is intended to be covered in one 45-minute session. The text contains some 60 of these document-lessons, thereby requiring the teacher to select, with the aid of the class, which areas, problems, or historical periods they wish to study.

Since a major thrust of this text is to effectuate appropriate and meaningful action by the class group, a final Projects and Activities Appendix is provided to serve as a guide. The activities are intended to be done concurrently with the classroom study.

The material in this text has been arranged to be discussed in a classroom setting. Each of the four historical units surveying the Tsarist and Soviet periods, and the Introductory Unit containing contemporary Soviet Jewish statements, consists of a series of documents. These documents, taken from a variety of sources, were chosen to enable the student to analyze and examine their contents, and to form independent judgments about them. The introductions prior to each document and the "Questions to Consider" are intended to help place the material in perspective, and to suggest possible avenues of inquiry. It is not the intent of the author for the student to mechanically answer each of the questions as an exercise. Selectivity and class interest should be taken into consideration. Not all of the answers to the questions are to be found in this text. To that end, cross references have been provided to Salo Baron's *The Russian Jew Under Tsars and Soviets* (Macmillan Company, New York, 1964). The sources of documents quoted in the text are listed in the appendix. A selected bibliography for reference and future study is also included. The student is encouraged to develop and utilize these and other outside source material.

The documents in this collection were additionally chosen to stimulate the student to consider the contemporary American Jewish community, and his relationship to it. It is the belief of the author that by examining the historical and contemporary Russian Jewish community, the Jewish student of the 1970's can gain a greater understanding of his own roots, and can better shape the future of American Jewry.

The aim of this text is to develop within the student a sense of concern and a feeling of empathy for *K'lal Yisrael*: *K'lal Yisrael* in its vertical dimension—throughout Jewish history, and in its horizontal dimension—around the contemporary Jewish world. Spiritually we should dance with the Jews of Russia at *Simchat Torah;* we should have fought with the Partisans and have died at Babi Yar; we should "go up" to the *Kotel* in *Yerushalayim*. In the words of the rabbis, we should feel that: *"Kol Yisrael Arevim Zeh BaZeh"*—"The fate of the entire Jewish people is intertwined."

TABLE OF CONTENTS

A Word of Direction

INTRODUCTORY UNIT.... 1

Letters From Moscow	3
Letter From Soviet Georgia	10
The Jews of Silence	15
A Soviet Reply on Jews: No. 1	17
A Soviet Reply on Jews: No. 2	22

TSARIST JEWRY UNIT.... 26

The *Khazars*	27
Polish Jewry and the *Va'ad Arbah Ha'aratzot*	31
TaCH v'TahT and *The Slave*	33
The Slave: The *Mitzvah* of *Pidyon Shevuyim*	36
Chassidut	38
A Russian Jewish View of Secular Authority	44
The Russian Jews and the Draft	47
Into the Modern Age: The *Haskalah*	50
Into the Modern Age: Zionism	54
The Decline of Tsarist Jewry: The Kishinev Pogrom	57
The Decline of Tsarist Jewry: The Beilis Trial	62
A Prayer for the Tsar	65
The Jewish Population Explosion	68

SOVIET JEWRY UNIT
THE REVOLUTION UNTIL THE SHOAH.... 70

Soviet Jewry: An Overview	71
Ha'am	74

TABLE OF CONTENTS (continued)

"Vilna in Distress" 74
"The Election Campaign" 75
"The Separation of Church and State" 77
"The Revolution" 80
Jews in the Communist Party 82
Leon Trotsky and the Jews 85
The *Yevsektsiya* 88
Isaac Babel 91
The Soviet Jewish Economy 95
Soviet Jewish Book Publishing 97
Publishing in the Hebrew Language 100
The Pre-*Shoah* Soviet Jew 102

SOVIET JEWRY UNIT
The SHOAH.... 105

Einsatzgruppen 107
Russia at War 110
"Russo-Ukrainian Unity" 110
"The Liberation of Maidanek: A Polish Reaction" ... 111
"The Liberation of Maidanek: The Russian Reaction".. 113
The Jewish Anti-Fascist Committee 115
Jewish Resistance: The Partisans 118
The Blackbook 122
The *Mitzvah* of Remembering 125

SOVIET JEWRY UNIT
The Black Years and Contemporary Soviet Jewry.... 127

The Black Years: Golda Meir in Moscow 128
The Black Years: The "Doctor's Plot" 131
Post-War Soviet Yiddish Publishing 134
The Use of Yiddish in the Soviet Union 136

TABLE OF CONTENTS (*continued*)

Soviet Jewry in the 1960's: "Babi Yar" 138
Soviet Jewry in the 1970's: Jewish Activists Challenge
    the Soviet Government 142
The Education Tax 145
Russian Jewish Emigration 148
A Model Jewish Community 152
The Russian Jewish Community 153
Class Trip to the Soviet Union 157
Afterward 162

APPENDIX—PROJECTS AND REVIEW 163

I. Classroom Learning Projects 165
II. Community Educating Projects 167
III. Community Activating Projects 171
Self-Test Review 177

BIBLIOGRAPHY 184

SOURCES 190

JEWS IN RUSSIA:
THE LAST FOUR CENTURIES

Introductory Unit

It is difficult to focus on a clear image of the three million Jews of the Soviet Union. Geographically spread from as far flung regions of the USSR as Bukhara in Central Asia and Riga on the Baltic Sea, to Birobidzhan in eastern Siberia; religiously observant, non-observant, or anti-observant; politically identified with the ruling Communist Party, the Zionist movement, or neither; highly urbanized and educated; the Soviet Jew, as the average American Jew, takes on any one of a number of multiple personalities. How then are we to proceed in somehow meeting, understanding, and identifying with these three million Jews? We have to listen to their voices, read their words, and often, hear their cries.

Soviet Jewry does not speak with a single voice. Different age groups, political affiliations, geographical localities and religious backgrounds express their own unique feelings. In this Introductory Unit we will hear from the young and the old, the Communist and the Zionist, the discontented and the satisfied. We will travel from the streets of Soviet Georgia to the streets of Moscow, attend a press conference in Moscow, and hear from a ranking Jewish Communist official.

2   JEWS IN RUSSIA: LAST FOUR CENTURIES

In addition to the material provided in this textbook, *The Jews of Silence* by Elie Wiesel will be assigned as outside reading.

Much of the classroom discussion will depend upon your current involvement with the problems of Soviet Jews. You are encouraged to share with the class various newspaper clippings, magazine articles, and other similar sources from the daily press.

LETTERS FROM MOSCOW

For Soviet Jews, correspondence with the West entails taking many risks. Social pressure, loss of employment, expulsion from the university, political ostracism, and even arrest and imprisonment can result. Yet, since 1968, increasing numbers of Soviet Jews have written to the free world, sent messages out with visiting foreign tourists, or publicized them through various Soviet publications.

The following six letters were received in the West from a young Russian Jew, a university student in Moscow. The major language of the correspondence was Yiddish. The first letters begin with Zionist slogans in Hebrew.

April 15, 1969

Tov Lamud (sic) *Be'ad Artzeynu*
Dear Friend,

    Yesterday I received your letter which I have awaited for a long time. I was delighted to read your letter. I thank you many times for your remembering me and thank you very much. You ask what is new with me. I can write to you that there is no news at this time. It is already the fifth month since we have turned in all the papers in the government office, since receiving from my mother's sister a visa. ... But we have received no answer.

    Before you realize it, the happy holiday of *Pesach* is already passed, and I want to wish you health and good life.

    I believe in that what is written in the last line of the *Seder* will come to pass this year.

It would be very interesting if you could write more of life in Israel.

I have for you not a great request. I ask you to send me a few pictures of soldiers from *Tzahal* (Israel Defense Army).

I conclude my short note and I await anxiously for your answer.

Shalom,
Boris

April 17, 1969

Shalom dear Friend,

I was very glad to receive your letter and I have already answered it. But I have decided to write this postcard because I am not sure if you have received that letter. I want to ask you to send me the postcards without an envelope and by airmail.

Many thanks for your care of me.

Shalom,
Boris

Questions to Consider

1. What does the first letter tell us about the Jewish environment surrounding Boris?
2. What effects have 50 years of Soviet rule, and the last 20 years of repression in particular, had on his Jewish associations and identity?
3. Why does Boris make the request that he does?
4. How would you answer him? What moral and ethical considerations would you have to consider while dealing with his request?

INTRODUCTORY UNIT

Ahm Yisrael Chai!
                              June 12, 1969

Dear Friend,

   Today I received your two postcards. I had a lot of enjoyment from them. I have already written you that our entire family has given the papers to our government to leave for Israel. But for the present we have received no reply at all. We live with the hope. I gave you regards with one of my acquaintances. Please write me if he came to visit you. Did he speak to you about me?
   I thank you because you have not forgotten me, and think of me. I want to hear an answer from you.

                              Warm Regards,
                              BORIS

Questions to Consider

1. What is the nature of Boris' request to the Soviet government? What is the current status of his request?
2. How long does it take to get a passport in the U.S.? How long has Boris been waiting?
3. In your opinion, what is Boris' major concern in writing?

                              June 22, 1969

Dear Friend,

   I didn't wait to hear but I am writing a few words. A few days ago they refused us permission to go to our own land. You should yourself understand what a great problem it was for us. My mother hasn't seen her sister in many years.
   I would certainly want to write you all about all of our great problems but I haven't lost my hope that He will listen to our prayers. Not looking on all of our problems we have

a hope to travel to *Aretz*. I have a hope that you in time, as one of my own, will help us too.

I am ending my letter with a heartfelt regards from all of us. Am waiting for an answer.

BORIS

Questions to Consider

1. What is your initial reaction to Boris' letter?
2. To what kinds of "problems" is he referring? What consequences can befall Russian citizens requesting permission to go to Israel?
3. Why does Boris address the person to whom he writes as "one of my own"? To what is he referring?

July 6, 1969

Dear Friend,

I didn't wait for your letter and am writing you a few words. I already wrote you in the previous letter that to come to Israel presents for us a lot of difficulties. But we believe that the Master of the World would not forsake us, and his children will gather together on our land.

Nothing new by me, except that with all my memories and my whole heart is with you, and more in life one doesn't need. Only to come to you and to live a free life.

I hope to meet you on a trip to *Aretz*.

A warm heartfelt regards from my family.

BORIS

Questions to Consider

1. How does the tone of this letter differ from the previous ones?

2. What are the chief concerns of Boris about the Jews outside of the Soviet Union? What does he feel and hope about us?

The two weeks between Boris' letters of June 22 and July 6 were ones of great personal crisis and decision.

The following letter was written on June 25, 1969. The signers were branded as "enemies of the Soviet state," and were placed under close surveillance. Boris was held for three months in a Russian Secret Police prison in Moscow.

To: The Chairman of the Council of Ministers of the USSR, A. Kosygin
From: Citizens U. I. Klaizmer, B. I. Borukhovich, and Boris Shlein, Moscow, Zh. 457, Pervaya Novokuzminskaya, Apt. 72

OPEN LETTER

In view of the fact that our many letters, statements and appeals to you personally, as well as to other highly placed Soviet statesmen, have met with no response, we have decided to turn with this letter to those press organs that will understand the tragedy of our situation and will agree to publish this letter.

We, the undersigned, constitute one family and are Jews by nationality. On December 30, 1968, basing ourselves upon the formal affidavit of invitation from our sisters, we applied for exit permits to the State of Israel in order to be reunited with close relatives from whom we were separated as a result of the War and whom we have not seen for thirty years. On June 16, 1969, our application was denied, our natural human urge to live with our closest relatives, with our people and in the land of our people was rejected.

We consider the fact that our request was under consideration for nearly six months only to be rejected, as an appalling act of mocking humiliation and anti-Semitism.

Our family was educated in the tradition of Jewish culture, but in the present conditions of Soviet reality our children are denied the possibility of learning their own language, as well as the great cultural heritage and all the spiritual values of our people, because unlike other peoples living in the USSR, the Jewish people is subjected to cruel discrimination. There exist in the USSR neither Jewish schools nor any other Jewish institutions of learning nor theaters since the bloody repressions of 1948-1953; there exist no periodical Jewish publications except one lone magazine.

Absolutely everything connected with the achievement of the Jewish people's philosophers and men of culture, science and art, everything connected with the heroism of the Jewish people and the sufferings it experienced—everything Jewish, in short, is silenced.

Books by a writer like Kichko, informed with a consistent and open anti-Semitic spirit on the level of the propaganda of the Czarist Black Hundreds, are published and popularized. All this profoundly insults our national feelings and our human dignity, and to remain in such an atmosphere of anti-Semitic propaganda and discrimination is unbearable to us.

We feel ourselves to be Jews emotionally and spiritually, bound up with our Jewish State of Israel. As free men who have committed no crimes, in full consonance with the Constitution of the USSR as well as with the basic principles of the (U.N.) Convention on the Elimination of All Forms of Racial Discrimination, and in accordance with the statement you made at a press conference in Paris in December, 1966, we have the full right of emigrating to Israel. We would like to hope that you will reveal understanding and that our requests will be complied with.

(signed) Klaizmer
Borukhovich
Shlein*

* NOTE: Because of worldwide publicity, Boris and his family were allowed by the Soviet authorities to emigrate to Israel in June, 1971.

1. How does Boris describe "the present conditions of Soviet reality?" In what major areas are Jewish rights infringed.

2. What compelled his family to publish this letter?

3. In the United States, how would we publicly register a similar protest? Why can't they act similarly?

4. What can we do to help families and individuals who have taken such risks in publicly announcing their desire to leave the Soviet Union? Which avenues of action would be most meaningful and effective?

LETTER FROM SOVIET GEORGIA

The Jews of Soviet Georgia represent a unique community within Soviet Jewry. Numbering some 80,000, they have maintained the traditional religious practices of the Jewish people. *Kashrut*, the observance of the *Shabbat*, and other *Mitzvot*, are widespread. Above all, their tie to the Land of Israel as the Jewish homeland is intense and passionate.

A number of factors serve to explain their relative freedom. Having been among the original settlers in the Caucasus, they lack the foreignness of the Jews in the Russian Republic. Their Sephardic customs and traditions tend to foster stronger ethnic and religious bonds. The percentage of Russians who have moved there is among the lowest of any of the member republics of the Soviet Union. Since that area of the Caucasus was not invaded by the Nazis, the indigenous community remains strong. The fact that Stalin himself came from this region also explains why it maintained its special status.

The following letter was first publicized by Prime Minister Golda Meir in the Knesset in Jerusalem in August, 1969. It requests the Government of Israel to make its contents available to the member nations of the United Nations, and to the world press, complete with the list of signers and their addresses. The covering letter to Golda Meir closes with the following statement:

> *"For the time of fear has passed—the hour for action has come.*

INTRODUCTORY UNIT

*For if I am not for myself, then who will be for me?
And if not now, then—when?"*

To the Commission on Human Rights
United Nations
New York, USA

We, eighteen religious Jewish families of Georgia, request you to help us leave for Israel. Each one of us, upon receiving an invitation from a relative in Israel, obtained the necessary questionnaires from the authorized USSR agencies, and filled them out. Each was assured orally that no obstacles would be put in the way of his departure. Expecting to receive permission any day, each sold his property and gave up his job. But long months have gone by—years, for many—and permission for departure has not yet been given. We have sent hundreds of letters and telegrams; they have vanished like tears in the sand of the desert. All we hear are one-syllable oral refusals. We see no written replies. No one explains anything. No one cares about our fate.

But we are waiting, for we believe in God.

We eighteen religious Jewish families of Georgia consider it necessary to explain why we want to go to Israel.

Everybody knows how justly national policy, the theoretical principles of which were formulated long ago by the founder of the State, V. I. Lenin, is in fact being carried out in the USSR. There have not been pogroms, Pales, or quotas in the country for a long, long time. Jews can walk the streets without fear for their lives; they can live where they wish, hold any position, even as high as the post of minister, as is evident from the example of V. Dymshits, Deputy Chairman of the USSR Council of Ministers. There is even a Jewish deputy in the Supreme Soviet—A. Chakovsky, Editor-in-Chief of *Literaturnaya Gazeta*.

Therefore, it is not racial discrimination that compels us to leave the country. Then perhaps it is religious discrimination?

But synagogues are permitted in the country, and we are not prohibited from praying at home. However, our prayers are with Israel, for it is written: 'If I forget thee, O Jerusalem, may my right hand forget its cunning." For we religious Jews feel that there is no Jew without faith, just as there is no faith without traditions. What, then, is our faith and what are our traditions?

[He describes the destruction of the Temple in the year 70, and the exile] . . . and whoever survived, reached other countries, to believe, and pray and wait.

Henceforth they had to find a way to live in alien lands among people who hated them. Showered with insults, covered with mud of slander, despised and persecuted, they earned their daily bread with blood and sweat, and reared their children.

Their hands were calloused, their souls drenched in blood. But the important thing is that the nation was not destroyed —and what a nation.

The Jews gave the world religion and revolutionaries, philosophers and scholars, wealthy men and wise men, geniuses with hearts of children, and children with eyes of old people. There is no field of knowledge, no branch of literature and art, to which Jews have not contributed their share. There is no country which gave the Jews shelter which has not been repaid by their labor. And what did the Jews get in return? . . .

Who didn't persecute the Jews! Everybody joined in baiting them.

When untalented generals lost a war, those to blame for the defeat were found at once—Jews. When a political adventurer did not keep the mountains of promises he had given, a reason was found at once—the Jews. Jews died in the torture chambers of the Inquisition in Spain, and in fascist concentration camps in Germany. Anti-Semites raised a scare—in enlightened France it was the Dreyfus case; in illiterate Russia, the Beiliss case.

And the Jews had to endure everything. . . .

Their blood is in our veins, and our tears are their tears.

The prophecy has come true: Israel has risen from the ashes; we have not forgotten Jerusalem, and it needs our hands.

There are eighteen of us who signed this letter. But he errs who thinks that there are only eighteen of us. There could have been many more signatures.

They say there is a total of twelve million Jews in the world. But he errs who believes there is a total of twelve million of us. For with those who pray for Israel are hundreds of millions who did not live to this day, who were tortured to death, who are no longer here. They march shoulder to shoulder with us, unconquered and immortal, those who handed down to us the traditions of struggle and faith.

That is why we want to go to Israel. . . .

It is incomprehensible that in the twentieth century people can be prohibited from living where they wish to live. It is strange that it is possible to forget the widely publicized appeals about the right of nations to self-determination—and, of course, the right of the people who comprise that nation.

We will wait months and years, we will wait all our lives, if necessary, but we will not renounce our faith or our hopes.

We believe: our prayers have reached God.

We know: our appeals will reach people.

For we are asking—let us go to the land of our forefathers. (the signatures of the eighteen families in the Soviet Georgian towns of Kutaisi, Poti, Tbilisi, and Kulashi follow).

Questions to Consider

1. What complaints do these families have against the Soviet Union? How is their letter different from that of the Shlein family of June 25, 1969?

2. According to this letter, what ties all Jews together? Why is Israel so important to them? Do you agree with their analysis of Jewish history?

3. Russian Jews have asked American Jewish travelers to the USSR: "We can not go to Israel—yet you in America are free: Why don't the Jews of the United States move to Israel?" How would you respond?

THE JEWS OF SILENCE

With its publication in 1966, *The Jews of Silence* by Elie Wiesel (Holt, Rinehart, and Winston, New York, 1966) was the first book to awaken the American Jewish Community to the situation of the Jews in the Soviet Union. His descriptions of Jewish celebration in Moscow, and of the nature of the existing communal life, reached a very wide audience, both Jewish and non-Jewish alike. Even now, the narrative remains one of the most poignant and powerful expressions of personal experiences with Soviet Jews.

The author was born in Hungary in 1928. Deported to concentration camps during the Holocaust, he survived Auschwitz, and made his way to Paris, Israel, and currently resides in New York City. His more than ten other books, plus numerous articles and publications, rank him among the world's leading Jewish authors.

Read *The Jews of Silence* for your own pleasure. The following questions will help in focusing your attention on some of the major aspects of the book.

1. Why did Wiesel travel to the Soviet Union? Would you make a similar trip? Have you come in contact with any of your contemporaries who have followed in Elie Wiesel's footsteps? How do their experiences compare with his 1966 narrative?

2. Which scene or vignette most impressed you from the book?

3. How would you describe the situation of the Jews in

the Soviet Union as seen through the eyes of Elie Wiesel? How does he describe the young people in Russia?

4. How would you define the concept of *"K'lal Yisrael?"* What does it mean to the Jews of the Soviet Union? What does it mean to you?

5. Subsequent to the publication of this book, Wiesel wrote the following:

"If I shall ever be remembered, it will be because of one sentence I coined: The Jews of Silence. Unfortunately, like many of the sentences I wrote, this one too was misinterpreted or misunderstood. The Jews of silence were not the Jews in Russia, but the. . . ."

How would you finish the sentence? Who are the Jews of Silence to whom Elie Wiesel referred? Why are they silent? How would you break their silence?

A SOVIET REPLY ON JEWS: NO. 1

Not all Soviet Jews want to go to Israel. Many undoubtedly are loyal to the current regime in the Soviet Union, and support the Soviet state's position concerning Zionism and the Middle East conflict.

Zionism has long been in disfavor in the USSR. Following the revolution of 1917, the Zionist Party was declared illegal, and all of its activities and programs were ordered halted. The study of the Hebrew language was discouraged, and in recent years has been grounds for accusing Soviet Jews of "anti-Soviet propaganda."

The outstanding success of the Israeli Army, especially in the Six-Day War, only further served to incense the Soviet regime. The concerted support of the USSR for the various Arab countries makes Jewish allegiance to Israel almost treasonable.

In February and March, 1970, in a series of public press conferences and statements, leading Soviet Jews assailed Zionism and supported the Soviet policy in the Middle East.

The following are taken from news reports as they appeared in the *New York Times*:

ZIONISM ASSAILED BY MOSCOW RABBI

By James F. Clarity
Special to the *New York Times*

MOSCOW, Feb. 28—The Chief Rabbi of Moscow came out today in support for the campaign against Zionism and Israel.

"There is no doubt," the Rabbi said in *Izvestia,* "that in certain circles in the U.S.A., mainly among big capitalists and rich Jews, it would be disadvantageous if the Jewish workers in America knew the truth about the Soviet Union.

"American Jews visiting the Soviet Union," the Rabbi said, "could see that they were being spoon-fed with Zionist propaganda, the basest lies." The Rabbi said that during his visit to the United States in 1968, he was asked by an Israeli diplomat in Washington, "Is there anti-Semitism in the U.S.S.R.?"

The Rabbi said he had answered the question by reminding the diplomat of the maltreatment and pogroms of Jews in Russia under the Czars. He said many Jews, under the Soviet regime, had become scientists and artists, while under Czarism they would have been restricted to menial occupations.

"And only the revolution in Russia, only Soviet power, opened to them all the roads to happiness equal to citizens of any other nationality of our country," the Rabbi said.

SOVIET JEWS, AT A NEWS PARLEY, BACK MOSCOW'S MIDEAST POLICY

By Bernard Gwertzman
Special to the *New York Times*

MOSCOW, March 4—Dozens of prominent Soviet Jews appeared at a Government-sponsored news conference today and pledged loyalty to Moscow's policy while condemning Israel, Zionism, and the United States.

As the Soviet Union stepped up its anti-Israel campaign, the Jews stood under glaring lights and described as lies Western accusations that Jews were discriminated against in the Soviet Union. They said their life was better than that of Jews living in the United States.

Those present included Veniamin E. Dymshits, a Deputy Premier; Arkady Raikin, comedian; and Academicians Gersh J. Budker, physicist; Isaak I. Mints, historian, and Mark B. Mitin, philosopher.

Today's statement said:

"Every day brings new reports about the crimes of the Israeli military, reviving memories of the barbarity of Hitlerites. This aggression has become a component part of the imperialist, neocolonialist plot directed against the people and progressive regimes of the Middle East, and closely intertwining the interests of oil monopolies and international Zionist operations."

"Zionism has always expressed the chauvinistic views and racist ravings of the Jewish bourgeoisie. It has not reached the apogee in preaching national intolerance and hatred. Zionists supply imperialism with cannon fodder in the struggle against the Arab peoples."

Deputy Premier Dymshits was the most active participant in the question-and-answer period. Waving a copy of the Soviet Constitution, he said that Jews were protected against discrimination by the Constitution and that no other country gave Jews such protection.

Iosif L. Bokor, the First Deputy Chairman of the Jewish Autonomous Region, conceded that there were no Yiddish schools in his area "because no one wants any," and proudly waved a copy of the region's single-page Yiddish newspaper to show that culture was alive there. Only about 15,000 of the Soviet Union's 3 million Jews live in the region, set up about 1930 in the Soviet Far East.

(The full list of 52 signatories follows.)

SOVIET CAMPAIGN JOINED BY RABBIS

By Bernard Gwertzman
Special to the *New York Times*

MOSCOW, March 9—Eleven Soviet lay Jews added their names to the campaign against Israel and Zionism, declaring that "the real motherland of Soviet Jews is our native Soviet Union."

Moscow's chief rabbi, Yehuda-Leib Levin, was one of those who signed today's statement. Earlier in the campaign the rabbi had denounced Zionism in an interview with a Moscow newspaper. Other signers included Rabbi A. R. Lubanov of Leningrad, Rabbi G. I. Mizrakhi of Baku, Rabbi I. B. Shvartsbladt of Odessa, Rabbi M. Z. Oppenshtein of Kubishev, and Rabbi I. S. Livsshits of Novozybkov.

Alluding to statements charging that Jews were not permitted to emigrate to Israel, the rabbis said:

"We wish to say to those maligners: the real motherland of Soviet Jews is our native Soviet Union. Like members of other ethnic groups, Jews have all the rights guaranteed by the Constitution, including the freedom of religious worship. The peoples of our country live as brothers, and no one will be able to sow discord among them."

Questions to Consider

1. On what bases do the speakers object to Israel and Zionism? How would you respond to them?

2. What could you suggest as possible motives to some of the signers of these declarations? Do you believe that they all agree with what they are signing?

3. Have you ever been under pressure to agree with something about which you had serious hesitations or disagreements? Under what circumstances?

4. Where is the "real motherland" of American Jews: the United States or Israel, neither, or both?

5. Have there been other cases of Jews publicly attacking Israel or other Jewish causes? In your opinion when is this justified, if ever?

6. In late 1971, the Chief Rabbi of Moscow's Archipova Street synagogue died at the age of 77. If you would have had to deliver his eulogy, what would you have said?

7. Following these reports, on March 10, 1970, 39 Soviet Jews came out publicly against the Soviet government's anti-Israel stance. They declared: "We believe that Jews will answer the anti-Israel campaign not by renunciation but by fortifying their pride in their people and exclaiming Next Year in Jerusalem."

How do you account for these divergent views? In your opinion, who speaks for the Jews of the Soviet Union? On what do you base your answer?

A SOVIET REPLY ON JEWS: NO. 2

The attention of the world press became focused on the condition of the Jews of the Soviet Union in the wake of a series of trials conducted in major Russian cities in 1970 and 1971. The Soviet government had charged a group of Jews with the attempted hijacking of a Soviet aircraft. Additionally, increased Soviet Jewish militancy in the forms of letters to the West, petitions to the Soviet government, applications for exit visas, and even a "sit-in" in the Kremlin, had stimulated a wide Jewish and non-Jewish response in the free world.

Faced with such a negative public image, one of the Soviet government's responses took the form of a letter from a leading Jewish Communist to the *New York Times* (May 21, 1971). Aron Vergelis, a Soviet Yiddish poet, is the editor of the only Yiddish language magazine published in the USSR, the monthly *Sovetish Heymland*.

> MOSCOW—It is with more than a little astonishment that I read tales in the American press about the "plight" of Jews in the Soviet Union. There is no freedom of religion, Jewish culture is suppressed, great masses of Soviet Jews clamor to leave their homeland for Israel and so on *ad nauseum.*
>
> I often wonder: Are the authors of these tales really talking about the Soviet Union?
>
> What they say has no relation whatsoever to the facts, to put the matter most politely. Why then are these tales concocted?

INTRODUCTORY UNIT 23

Take the canard that Jewish culture is suppressed. I happen to have some familiarity with this question as a writer of Jewish descent and as the chief editor of a Yiddish cultural publication, who has lived all his life in the Soviet Union, quite happily, thank you.

As readers of *The New York Times* should know, the Soviet Union is a multinational state. Soviet citizens of Jewish descent have made and are making a most worthy contribution.

I do not know how many literary works are published in Yiddish in the United States, but judging from what I hear, they are very, very few in number. In the Soviet Union, which has a considerably smaller Jewish population than does the United States, writers of Jewish descent, who choose to write in Yiddish, publish numerous books annually.

I understand that in the United States the Yiddish theater has died out. In the Soviet Union there are Jewish theatrical companies, both professional and amateur, in Vilnius, Kaunas, Kishinev, Dvinsk, Birobidjan, and elsewhere. Yiddish songs are recorded and widely distributed on gramaphone discs.

And then, there is the canard, uncritically swallowed by some Americans, that great numbers of Soviet Jews ardently desire to leave their homeland and to settle in Israel because of Zionist sentiments.

May I assure my readers that I have attempted to make a thorough study of these allegations and found them completely groundless. First, only a relatively insignificant number of Soviet Jews apply for permits to go to Israel; second, most of these applications are motivated by the desire for reunion with relatives.

The Zionist tale that the Soviet Government prevents Jews from going to Israel is patently absurd. Not long ago a high Israeli official stated that about a thousand Jews annually emigrate from the Soviet Union to Israel. Despite the absence of diplomatic relations between the Soviet Union and Israel,

Soviet Jews who wish to go to Israel can do so—not, of course, by hijacking airplanes.

That the number of such Jews is very small simply testifies to the truth that the vast majority of Jews in the Soviet Union are devoted to the same lofty socialist ideals as the other peoples of the Soviet Union and totally reject the pretensions of Zionism.

And this brings me back to the question I originally raised: What motivates the current Zionist barrage of anti-Soviet fabrications and the shouts about "Soviet anti-Semitism."

The root cause, I believe, is the crisis of Zionism itself, stemming from its ideological and political failures. The leaders of Zionism had hoped to draw to Israel, Jewish people from all corners of the world. But this was a wild dream that failed.

The intensification of Zionism's anti-Soviet campaign is timed with a view to the 28th world Zionist congress scheduled to take place at the end of this year. One of the goals of the congress is to raise a billion dollars for Israel to enable it to continue its course of aggression.

Whether these Americans are really to be milked by the organizers of the congress is their business. But as a Soviet citizen and as the editor of a Soviet Jewish literary publication, I feel impelled to register my indignation at the anti-Soviet canards that are being fabricated in this connection.

Questions to Consider

1. How does Vergelis respond to the claims that Soviet Jews are culturally deprived, and wish to move to Israel? How would you answer Vergelis' position?

2. What is Vergelis' assessment of the success of the Zionist movement? What does being a "Zionist" signify to you? Are you a Zionist?

3. For whom does Vergelis speak—for some, all, or none, of the Soviet Jews?

4. What, in fact, is the spirit of the Jews in the Soviet Union? Is it better represented by the letters of the Shlein family and the eighteen families from Soviet Georgia, or more like the position outlined by Aron Vergelis and the Moscow press conferences? How would you weigh each of the statements, and come to a definitive answer?

5. If you were now living in the Soviet Union, with which position would you identify, and why?

Tsarist Jewry Unit

INTRODUCTION

The Russian Jewish community has its roots deep into the time and soil of Eastern Europe. It extends back some ten centuries in history, and comes as the heir and remnant of a once great and flourishing Polish Jewish community.

In this unit we shall span a thousand years of Jewish history in Eastern Europe, and focus on a number of selected problems: the *Khazar* epic, the rise and fall of Polish Jewry, *Chassidut*, the Jewish view of the Tsar, the Tsarist policy towards the Jews, internal Jewish developments including the Enlightenment and Zionism, the pogroms, the Beilis trial, and the Jewish population explosion.

In addition to the sources provided in this textbook, *The Slave* by Isaac Bashevis Singer should also be read. *The Russian Jew Under Tsars and Soviets* by Salo W. Baron (Macmillan, N.Y.C., 1964) is highly recommended as a reference work. It will serve to fill in much of the detail which has not been included in this book. References to the appropriate pages in Baron are included.

THE *KHAZARS*

The earliest traces of Jewish settlement in the area now known as Russia or the Soviet Union came through Black Sea trade routes from the Mediterranean Sea. Greek synagogue inscriptions dating from the beginning of the common era have been discovered in the Black Sea area. Second century Hebrew inscriptions were also found in the Crimea. These point to the presence of organized Jewish communities within this corner of the ancient Roman Empire.

In the eighth century, the ruling classes of a kingdom to the north of the Black Sea, in what is now the southern Ukraine, converted to Judaism. Although the historical records of this land Khazaria, as the Jewish state was called, are clouded by time, other Jewish communities did establish contact with it.

Hasdai Ibn Shaprut of tenth century Islamic Spain served in the royal court of Abd-Al-Raham III as physician, inspector-general of customs and diplomatic advisor. He was known as an extremely able diplomat, and was credited with having established favorable political relations between Spain, and Byzantium, and neighboring Christian lands.

During Ibn Shaprut's service he heard news of the existence of the Jewish kingdom, and sent a letter to its ruler Joseph the King of the *Khazars*.

The text of the letter is as follows:

> I, Hasdai, son of Isaac, son of Ezra, belonging to the exiled Jews of Jerusalem in Spain, a servant of my lord the King,

bow to the earth before him and prostrate myself toward the abode of your Majesty. I rejoice in your tranquility and magnificence and stretch forth my hands to God in heaven that He may protect and prolong your reign in Israel. . . .

Praise be to the beneficent God for His mercy towards me! Kings of the earth, to whom his magnificence and power are known, bring gifts to him conciliating his favor by costly presents, such as the King of the Franks, the King of the Gebalim, who are Germans, the King of Constantinople, and others. All their gifts pass through my hands, and I am charged with making gifts in return. . . .

I always ask the ambassadors of these monarchs who bring gifts, about our brethren, the Israelites, the remnant of the captivity, whether they have heard anything concerning the deliverance of those who have languished in bondage and have found no rest.

At length mercantile emissaries of Khorasan told me that there is a kingdom of Jews which is called Al-Khazar. But I did not believe these words for I thought they told me such things to procure my goodwill and favor. I was therefore wondering till the ambassadors of Constantinople came with presents and a letter from their king to our king, and I interrogated them concerning this matter.

They answered me: It is quite true, and the name of that kingdom is Al-Khazar. It is fifteen days journey by sea from Constantinople, but by land many nations intervene between us; the name of the king now reigning is Joseph; ships sometimes come from their country to ours bringing fish, skins, and wares of every kind. The men are our confederates and are honored by us; there is communication between them and us by embassies and mutual gifts; they are powerful; they maintain numerous armies with which they occasionally engage in expeditions.

When I heard this report I was encouraged, my hands

For further background, cf. Baron, pp. 3-4.

were strengthened, and my hope was confirmed. Thereupon I bowed down and adored the God of heaven.

(He asks the King to explain in detail the rise of his kingdom, being anxious to find out whether there is anywhere a soil and a kingdom where scattered Israel is not subject and subordinate to others.)

Were I to know that this is true I should renounce my place of honor, abandon my lofty rank, forsake my family, and wander over mountains and hills, by sea and on land, until I reached the dwelling place of my Lord and sovereign, there to behold his greatness and splendor, the seats of his subjects, the position of his servants, and the tranquility of the remnant of Israel. . . .

Having been cast down from our former glory, and now living in Exile, we are powerless to answer those who constantly say unto us: Every nation has its own kingdom while you have no trace of a kingdom on earth. But when we received the news about our lord and sovereign, about the power of his kingdom and the multitude of his hosts, we were filled with astonishment. We lifted our heads, our spirit was revived, and our hands were strengthened, the kingdom of my lord serving us as an answer. Would that this rumor might be verified, for thereby will our greatness be enhanced!

I pray for the health of my lord the king, of his family, and of his house, and that his throne may be established for ever. Let his days and his sons' days be prolonged in the midst of Israel!

Questions to Consider

1. What light does this letter shed on the position of the Jews in Spain at this time? How had they achieved such prominence? Who are some of the other figures associated with this period in Jewish history?

2. How did Ibn Shaprut use his position to aid Jewish causes? Is it proper for Jewish officials to use their position to further Jewish interests? What kinds of considerations are involved in making such a decision?

3. Would your reaction be the same as Ibn Shaprut's to hearing of the existence of such a Jewish kingdom? Would you be willing to move there?

4. What was the fate of the *Khazar* kingdom?

5. A number of American Jews have served as leading presidential advisors in recent times, including Bernard Baruch, Arthur Goldberg, Abe Fortas, and Henry Kissinger. How would you account for this outstanding involvement of American Jews in such high positions? Did they achieve such rank only by virtue of personal qualities, or were their Jewish backgrounds somehow involved?

POLISH JEWRY AND THE *VA'AD ARBAH HA'ARATZOT*

The expanding Kievan state soon conquered the *Khazars* in the mid-11th century, and was itself inundated by the Tartar invasions of Russia in the mid-13th century. To repopulate the ravaged lands of what is now the Ukraine, Polish kings encouraged the migration of Jewish and Christian merchants, traders, artisans, and craftsmen, who laid the foundation for a Polish middle class. The reign of King Casimir the Great (1333-1370) further extended Jewish settlement in such towns as Cracow, Lvov, and Lublin.

The Polish Jewish Community grew in size and importance, numbering at the end of the 16th century 500,000. Meanwhile the Muscovite (later Russian) empire refused to allow any Jewish settlement, and with few exceptions, Russia was empty of Jews until the later half of the 18th century. Internal autonomy was granted to the Jews of Poland, culminating in the organization of the *Va'ad Arbah Ha-Aratzot*, the Council of the Four Lands (the Jewish communities of Great Poland, Little Poland, "Russia," and Volhynia) at the end of the 16th century. The *Va'ad* exercised religious, economic, and political control over the Jews, and functioned virtually as a Jewish parliament until it went out of existence in 1764.

With this Jewish growth and renaissance, printed books on *Halacha* (Jewish law) and other religious themes gained wide circulation. Jewish presses sprang up all over Europe.

The following is an excerpt from a 1594 decision by the *Va'ad Arba Ha'Aratzot* concerning book publication and copyrights.

1. Books should not be printed without the permission of rabbis and leaders, and if a printer disregards this, then they will cancel the printing operation, and will boycott the printer, and all occupied with that work.

2. Books which are printed here (Cracow) or in Lublin are forbidden to be republished in Italy. And if they are printed there, they (officials of the *Va'ad*) should intervene with the heads of the lands, that they should not be sold until after a given period, and Italy should be told, and they (Italian Jewish printers) should negotiate here how much they will give on each page to the fund of the *Kahal* (the Jewish community). . . .

Questions to Consider

1. What does this indicate about the Jewish reading public in 16th century Poland and Italy?
2. What does this suggest about the scope and power of the *Va'ad?*
3. What "boycott" powers did the *Va'ad* possess? In what areas of life could their boycott be enforced?
4. Are there any American or world Jewish organizations which can speak with authority for all the nation's or the world's Jews? Which organizations do you consider to be your spokesmen?

TACH V'TAHT AND *THE SLAVE*

The greatness that was Polish Jewry was soon overwhelmed by disaster. In 1648, Ukrainian peasants led by the Cossack Bogdan Chmelnitsky broke into revolt, and began a ten year slaughter of Jews. The pogroms beginning in 1648-1649 caused the greatest Jewish suffering since the Crusades. This infamous period is known in Hebrew as *TaCH v'TahT* corresponding to its dates on the Jewish calendar (5408-5409).

The following two accounts bring different vantage points to this period of Jewish history. The first was written by a Russian historian, and the second by the foremost Jewish historian of the beginning of the 20th century, Simon Dubnov. Consult a Jewish historical atlas or a map of the Ukraine to locate the areas in question.

Assignment: For a most vivid reconstruction of this period read *The Slave* by Isaac Bashevis Singer.

> I. Killing was accompanied by barbarous tortures, the victims were flayed alive, split asunder, clubbed to death, roasted on coals, or scalded with boiling water. Even infants at the breast were not spared. The most terrible cruelty, however, was shown to the Jews. They were destined to utter annihilation, and the slightest pity shown to them was looked upon as treason. Scrolls of the Law were taken out of the synagogues and danced upon by the Cossacks while drinking whiskey. After this, Jews were laid down upon them, and butchered without mercy. Thousands of Jewish infants were thrown into wells, or buried alive.

II. The losses inflicted upon the Jews of Poland during the fatal decade of 1648-1658 were appalling. In the reports of chroniclers, the number of Jewish victims varies between one hundred thousand and five hundred thousand. But even if we accept the lower figure, the number of victims still remains colossal, excelling the catastrophes of the Crusades and the Black Death in Western Europe. Some seven hundred Jewish communities in Poland had suffered massacre and pillage. In the Ukrainian cities situated on the left bank of the Dnieper, the Jewish communities had disappeared almost completely. In the localities on the right shore of the Dnieper, wherever the Cossacks had made their appearance, only about one-tenth of the Jewish population survived. The others had either perished during the rebellion of Chmelnitsky, or had been carried off by the Tartars into Turkey, or had emigrated into Lithuania, the central provinces of Poland, or the countries of Western Europe. All over Europe and Asia, Jewish refugees or prisoners of war could be met with, who had fled from Poland, or had been carried off by the Tartars, and ransomed by their brethren. Everywhere the wanderers told a terrible tale of the woes of their compatriots, and of the martyrdom of hundreds of Jewish communities.

Questions to Consider

1. Does the first description call to mind any other similar descriptions of Jewish suffering? Where and when?

2. Why do you think I. B. Singer posed his historical novel *The Slave* in the period of *TaCH v'TahT?*

3. There is a famous Hebrew story of a kibbutznik rising at a general meeting and exclaiming, "The Jews have no history—they *did* history to us!"

Who are the "they" in this incident? Do you agree or disagree with this statement?

How does Singer's story throw light on this question?

Do you believe that an American Jew would make such a statement today?

4. What is Singer's opinion about the status of the Jewish world of that period? What does he think about the leaders of the Jewish community?

5. If Singer were to pose this type of novel in the contemporary American Jewish scene, at which things would he look critically? At which things do you look critically?

THE SLAVE: THE *MITZVAH* OF *PIDYON SHEVUYIM*

In a story full of much ugliness, I. B. Singer reacts most favorably to the redemption of Yaakov. The religious aspects of this act were not lost on the Jews of that period, nor on Singer in telling his story. To many today, this *Mitzvah* of *Pidyon Shevuyim* (the ransom of captives) is the religious imperative for Jews to involve themselves in the problem and struggle of Soviet Jews.

For an insight into the importance of this *Mitzvah*, examine the following selection from the *Mishneh Torah* of the RaMBaM.

> The ransoming of captives has precedence over supporting and clothing the poor. There is no *Mitzvah* as great as that of ransoming captives, since the captive is in the category of those who are hungry, thirsty, and naked, and whose life stands in mortal danger. Moreover, he who ignores redeeming captives violates the following negative commands: Do not harden your heart nor shut your hand to your needy brother (Deuteronomy 15:7), Do not stand idly by the blood of your neighbor (Leviticus 19:16), Do not allow him to be ruled rigorously in your presence (Leviticus 25:53). He likewise denies the following positive commandments: And you shall surely open your hand to him (Deuteronomy 15:8), And your brother should live with you (Leviticus 25:36), Love your neighbor as yourself (Leviticus 19:18), and Save those who are taken to die (Proverbs 24:1), and many other similar commandments.

Truly, there is no *Mitzvah* greater than the ransoming of captives.

Questions to Consider

1. The RaMBaM identifies the *Mitzvah* of *Pidyon Shevuyim* with that of *Tsedakah*. What is the difference between "*Tsedekah*" and "charity?"
2. According to the reasoning of the RaMBaM, would it be permitted to violate the Shabbat to ransom a captive? In the view of the traditional *Halacha*, when is one allowed to violate even the Shabbat?
3. Why does the Jewish tradition put so much emphasis on the *Mitzvah* of *Pidyon Shevuyim?*
4. Do you know of any other examples in which attempts were made to trade money for Jewish lives? During the *Shoah?* In the modern day?
5. How can we fulfill this *Mitzvah* today? Regarding Jews in the USSR? Regarding Jews in Arab lands?

CHASSIDUT

In the wake of *TaCH v'TahT* (the destruction of 1648-49), in addition to great economic and physical destruction, the spirit of the Jewish nation had been severely challenged and stunned. Messianic hopefuls came and went, including the most famous of the false Messiahs, Shabbtai Tzvi. Feelings of frustration and depression overwhelmed the Jews of Eastern Europe.

At this very time of crisis, at the two corners of the Polish world, in Podolia in the south and Lithuania in the north, came a new spiritual regeneration. This resurgence is associated with two of the most charismatic and influential figures in Jewish history. They were the founder of the *Chassidic* movement Yisrael *Ba'al Shem Tov* (known as the *BeShT*), and Elijah, the spiritual and intellectual leader or *Gaon*, of Vilna.

The following selections are *Chasidic* tales in the name of the *Ba'al Shem Tov* and his disciples.

THE KADDISH OF LEVI YITZCHAK

Good morning to you Lord of the World!

I, Levi Yitzchak, son of Sarah of Berditchev, am coming to you in a legal matter concerning your people of Israel.

What do you want of Israel?

It is always: "Command the children of Israel." "Speak unto the children of Israel."

Merciful Father! How many peoples are there in the world?

The Russians—what do they say? Our emperor is the emperor!

The Germans—what do they say? Our kingdom is the kingdom!

The English—what do they say? Our empire is the empire!

But I, Levi Yitzchak, son of Sarah of Berditchev, say: I shall not go hence, nor budge from my place until there be a finish; until there be an end to exile—

"*Yisgadal veyishkadash shemay rabbah!*"

Questions to Consider

1. What is Levi Yitzchak's complaint to God? What does he request of God?

2. Does Levi Yitzchak expect his prayer to be answered? What effect does he believe his prayer will have?

3. What is the meaning of the concept "*Tikkun Olam*" (perfecting the world)? Where is it referred to in the daily prayers? Why is this concept so critical in *Chassidic* thought?

4. Is this concept of "*Tikkun Olam*" still viable today? Faced by a massive, technological civilization, by what kinds of acts can the individual hope to change or influence society?

5. Levi Yitzchak prays for an end to "exile." Exile from where? Are you in exile? What is the term for exile in Hebrew?

THE FIRE

When the great Rabbi Israel *Baal Shem Tov* saw misfortune threatening the Jews, it was his custom to go into a certain part of the forest to meditate. There he would light

---

For a description of the *Chassidic* movement and its leaders, see *Souls on Fire* by Elie Wiesel (Random House, New York, 1972).

a fire, say a special prayer, and the miracle would be accomplished and the misfortune averted.

Later when his disciple the celebrated Magid of Mezritch had occasion for the same reason to intercede with heaven, he would go to the same place in the forest and say: "Master of the universe, listen! I do not know how to light the fire but I am still able to say the prayer." Again the miracle would be accomplished.

Still later Rabbi Moshe Leiv of Sasov, in order to save his people once more, would go into the forest and say: "I do not know how to light the fire, I do not know the prayer, but I know the place, and this must be sufficient." And it was sufficient and the miracle was accomplished.

Then it fell to Rabbi Israel of Rizhyn to overcome misfortune. Sitting in his armchair, his head in his hands, he spoke to God: "I am unable to light the fire and I do not know the prayer; I cannot even find the place in the forest. All I can do is tell the story and this must be sufficient." And it was sufficient.

Questions to Consider

1. What place and influence did these men have in the *Chassidic* movement?

2. How would the students of the *Gaon* of Vilna have reacted to this story and to its approach? Why was the *Chassidic* movement so successful in reconstituting the nation after the destruction of 1648-49 and the onslaught of false Messianism?

3. How would you react if great misfortune were to confront the Jewish people and the world today? What kinds of options would you have open?

4. Is there a place for prayer in our contemporary world?

TSARIST JEWRY: AN OVERVIEW

With the partitions of Poland in the second half of the 18th century, the history of what we know today as Russian Jewry most properly begins. The following time chart provides a general framework for the status of Jewish life in Russia under the Tsars. Each of the four columns adds a different essential ingredient to the understanding of Tsarist Jewish life.

Assignment: In the first two columns ("Changes in Leadership" and "Wars") identify the dates given with specific events and personalities. For the last two columns ("Special Events" and "Jewish Events") be familiar with the significance of the happenings listed. The sequence and especially the correlation of events within a given period should be given special attention. The required information can be found in history textbooks and in Baron.

Changes in Leadership	Wars	Special Events	Jewish Events
1762			1760—Death of *BeShT*
	1768-		
		1772—Partition #1	
	1774		
			1791—Pale of Settlement Established
		1793—Partition #2	
		1795—Partition #3	
1796			
			1797—Death of Vilna *Gaon*
1801			

	1812-1814		1812—Death of Shneur Zalmon of Lyadi
		1815—Congress of Vienna	1817—Birth of Rabbi Isaac Elchanan Spektor
1825		1825—Decembrists	
			1827—Cantonists
	1830-31		
			1841—Crown Schools
1855	1853-1855		
			1859—Birth of Shalom Aleichem
		1861—Emancipation	1860—First Issue of *Rasvyet*
			1874—Birth of Weizmann
	1877-1878		
1881			1881—Wave of Pogroms 1881—"BILU"—First Modern Aliyah to Israel 1882—May Laws
1896			1897—Founding of Bund; First Zionist Congress 1903—Kishinev Pogrom
	1904-05	1905—Revolution	
	1914-1917		1913—Beilis Trial 1915—Pale Abolished

Questions to Consider

1. Which of the following were periods of relative liberalism in Tsarist Russia, and which were periods of relative repression?

TSARIST JEWRY UNIT 43

1764-1789 Rise of Catherine the Great—French Revolution
1790-1801 French Revolution—Death of Tsar Paul
1801-1812 Alexander I—Invasion of Napoleon
1815-1855 Victory Over Napoleon—Death of Nicholas I
1855-1866 Alexander II—Attempted Assassination on His Life
1866-1881 Assassination Attempt—Assassination of Alexander II
1881-1917 Alexander III and Nicholas II—Russian Revolution

2. In what ways did the various Tsars have different policies regarding the Jews? What was the lot of the Jews under the individual Tsars within these changing time periods?

3. What were the principles common to the approach of the Tsars regarding their treatment of the Jews?

4. What are the principles common to the approach of the Soviet government since 1917 regarding the Jews?

5. Which of the principles of the Soviet government have their genesis in the Tsarist period?

A RUSSIAN JEWISH VIEW OF SECULAR AUTHORITY

The invasion of Napoleon into Russia in 1812 posed the Jews of the Pale of Settlement with a great challenge and choice: whether to welcome the French emancipator of the Jews of Western Europe, or to support the Tsar, Alexander I. The tension involved in this choice was not only relevant then, but presents itself many times in Jewish history, particularly in the modern age.

The following folk tales about Napoleon in Jewish literature present their solution to this quandary.

>Rabbi Shneur Zalman of Lyadi was a member of the Russian war council and was attached to the general staff. He accompanied the armies on their campaigns. More than once he sat in headquarters, poring over a map and dictating strategic maneuvers. Many a tactical retreat was carried out according to his plan.
>
>When the Rabbi of Lyadi was freed from prison the French soldiers took him as a guide. The Rabbi was compelled to go and point out the roads to them. Therefore many rabbis in Russia took a dislike to Napoleon. Many rabbis, too, did not relish a victory of civilized France over Russia.
>
>In *Chassidic* circles it is related that Napoleon used to say: "Wherever I ride, that blond little Jew is before me" (Rabbi Shneur Zalman was red haired). It is said that the Rabbi used to appear to him and torment him.

There was a controversy between Rabbi Mendele of Rymanow and the Rabbi of Volozhin concerning Napoleon. The Rabbi of Volozhin even refused to call Napoleon "Emperor," merely "General." He used to say that our Tsar would win, much blood would be shed, but in return, mankind would be redeemed once and for all, and Jewish misfortune would come to an end.

Questions to Consider

1. According to these tales, whose side did the Jews take?
2. What objections to Napoleon do these folk tales raise?
3. Who was Rabbi Shneur Zalman of Lyadi? What was his place in the Chassidic movement? Why was he featured in these stories?
4. Consider the following statement by Rabbi Shneur Zalman: "Should Bonaparte win, the wealth of the Jews will be increased and their civil position will be raised. At the same time their hearts will be estranged from our Heavenly Father. Should, however, our Tsar Alexander win, the Jewish hearts will draw nearer to our Heavenly Father though the poverty of Israel may become greater and his position lower."

How does this help to explain the view of Napoleon taken by the legends? What was Napoleon's policy regarding the Jews of Western Europe, and why was Rabbi Shneur Zalman so opposed to it for Russian Jews?

5. Implicitly, what is Rabbi Shneur Zalman saying about Jewish survival? Under what conditions will Judaism best survive? Under what conditions will Judaism not survive?
6. Which view of Jewish survival was adopted in Eastern

For further background, cf. Baron, pp. 26-28.

Europe? Which view of Jewish survival was adopted in the United States?

7. Is the position maintained by Rabbi Shneur Zalman still viable in our community today? Why or why not?

8. If you had been in the entourage of Rabbi Shneur Zalman in 1812, what would you have advised him?

THE RUSSIAN JEWS AND THE DRAFT

Serving in the army has been a major problem and concern in Jewish life since Tsar Nicholas I decreed that Jews would have to join the Tsarist army for a 40 year term. The 1827 law fixed a rate of Jewish conscription 40% higher than that of non-Jews. The Tsar was quoted as having said that service in the army "will move them most effectively to change their religion."

The enforcement of this law was made the responsibility of the Jewish communal authorities. Hard pressed to fulfill their quotas, a number of communities resorted to extreme and by many standards, immoral, means to give the Tsar his due. Kidnappers roamed the Pale of Settlement looking for unattended or defenseless Jewish youths and children. Called *"Khappers"* in Yiddish, their reputation for infamy has come down as a central theme in Russian Jewish folklore and history. Very often the poor were forced to serve, while the rich managed not to be taken.

The following is an eyewitness account of the Jewish conscripted soldiers of Tsar Nicholas by the Russian intellectual and historian Alexander Herzen, in the mid-1830's.

> Pale, worn out, with frightened faces, they stood in thick, clumsy soldier's overcoats, with standup collars, fixing helpless, pitiful eyes on the garrison soldiers, who were roughly getting them into the ranks. The white lips, the blue rings under the eyes looked like fever or chill. And these sick children, without care or kindness, exposed to the icy wind

that blows straight from the Arctic Ocean, were going to their graves. . . . Boys of twelve or thirteen might somehow have survived, but little fellows of eight or ten. . . . No painting could reproduce the horror of that scene.

This Yiddish folk song of the period describes another aspect of the *"Khappers."*

> *Tots from school they tear away*
> *And dress them up in soldier's grey.*
> *And our leaders, and our rabbis,*
> *Do naught but deepen the abyss.*
> *Rich Mr. Rockover has seven sons,*
> *Not a one a uniform dons;*
> *But poor widow Leah has an only child,*
> *And they hunt him down as if he were wild.*
> *It is right to draft the hard-working masses;*
> *Shoemakers or tailors—they're only asses!*
> *But the children of the idle rich*
> *Must carry on, without a hitch.*

Questions to Consider

1. What options were open to the Jewish communal leaders of the mid-19th century in Russia other than compliance with the draft laws? How does this effect the morality of their actions?

2. During the *Shoah* (Holocaust) various Jewish communal leaders were faced with the dilemma of compliance with the Nazi authorities, or the results of non-compliance. What choice did the Jewish leaders usually favor? When did their position change? How would you explain the choice that they made?

For further background, cf. Baron, pp. 35-38.

3. How would you contrast and compare the two accounts of the Jewish children and the draft? What different problems and vantage points do they reflect?

4. Which classes of Jews in the Pale does the second quote present? How did this class division come to a head at the end of the century?

5. What contemporary American problem involving the Selective Service System does the second quote reflect?

6. How do the current draft system's exemptions and selections affect your life and those close to you?

INTO THE MODERN AGE: THE *HASKALAH*

Russia not only served as the genesis and home of many of the great social movements of the 20th century, as socialism and Zionism, but also as the fountainhead of outstanding religious and spiritual forces on the threshold of the modern age. Just as *Chassidut* and *Hitnagdut* came out of Vilna and the Ukraine, so too the Russian *Haskalah* (enlightenment) made a unique contribution to Jewish life.

The original enlightenment of Europe had begun in Germany in the 18th century, under the championship of Moses Mendelssohn and his followers. It fostered achievement and accomplishment in the non-Jewish world, and fought for civil rights. The traditionalists of the Jewish world were looked upon as backward and enslaved, living in ignorance. This German version of the enlightenment often led to assimilation, and to the Reform movement.

Russian *Haskalah*, however, moved in a different direction. It aimed at expanding the intellectual and social awareness of Russian Jewry within its own setting. Although dedicated to modernization and expansion of the intellect, the exponents of this movement used Jewish forms, such as Hebrew and Yiddish language periodicals and literature, to reach the masses.

Peretz Smolenskin (1842-1885) began his education in *Yeshivot* and *Chassidic* circles and soon turned to European languages and education. In 1869 he began to publish one of the first and most influential Hebrew journals *HaShachar*. Smolenskin's *Haskalah* repudiated assimilation and encouraged Jewish identity through Hebrew and love of Zion. It marked the turning point towards the development of the spirit of Jewish nationalism among the Russian Jewish community. Smolenskin saw the Jewish people as a national essence, even without a land, a language, or a government.

The following is a description of this Hebrew journal and the position of Smolenskin.

> *HaShachar*, the monthly which Smolenskin began to publish in the late sixties, was an extraordinary happening in the life of that Jewish intelligentsia which resisted the assimilatory currents and heeded the Hebrew word. For the Orthodox youth educated in the *yeshivas* and prayer houses, *HaShachar* was practically a revolutionary upheaval. Every copy in the hands of these young people was like a match put to a powder keg. *HaShachar* revolutionized their minds, undermined old ideas infested with traditional moldiness, and stimulated them to new ideas. It brought light into the most dismal Jewish byways, rescuing thousands of talented young people who otherwise would have exhausted their talents in sterile pastimes.
>
> This was why the fanatical guardians of traditional Jewry vented their wrath on *HaShachar* more than on other forbidden books. Woe to the *yeshiva* student caught with *HaShachar*. He took a drubbing, he suffered various indignities. Sometimes he was even expelled from the *yeshiva*. Yet despite their vigorous efforts, the officials of the *yeshiva* failed to bar *HaShachar*. When they chased it from one door, it came in through seven others. There was not one *yeshiva* in all the Russian Pale to which Smolenskin's *HaShachar* had not found its way. They read it on the *Gemmarah* and under the *Gemmarah* and sat up nights with it. Today this seems incredible. Yet the Orthodox considered *HaShachar*

as unclean, feeding on poison emanating from the anti-divine, while the young people looked upon it with piety and love, as something sacred.

This piety and love they conferred also on *HaShachar's* founder. They idealized and idolized Smolenskin. He became their symbol of beauty and ennoblement. They deluged him with letters about the problems that tormented them.

A wealthy Russian came to Vienna with his daughter to see Smolenskin. But in Vienna, by pre-arrangement, she met one of her Populist friends, and they fled to Switzerland. The father complained bitterly that Smolenskin, who taught everyone else wisdom, could not prevent his daughter's flight.

Smolenskin's answer was calm: "Not all fathers have heeded me. You, for example, who read *HaShachar* certainly ought to know my views. But how did you bring up your daughter? You had governesses and tutors, teaching her foreign languages. You sent her to high school, where she learned about other peoples. Did you teach her about our own people? Did you teach her our own language? Did you interest her in our own history? Did you want her to know about our own people and our own national aspirations? To whom, then, should you bring your complaints, if not to yourself?"

Questions to Consider

1. What does the title *HaShachar* mean? What does this indicate about the aspirations of Smolenskin and the *Haskalah*?

2. How much are we a product of our Jewish backgrounds, and how much of the general American culture? How would this proportion compare with the *Maskilim* (enlightened ones) of 19th century Russia?

For further background, cf. Baron, pp. 148-157, 172-173.

3. What is the place of spoken and written Hebrew in contemporary American Jewish society and culture? In your opinion, what is the future of Hebrew outside of Israel?

4. What is Smolenskin's answer to assimilation and intermarriage? How successful a solution is it? Can you bring personal examples of individuals for whom this has or has not been a satisfactory answer?

5. Which are the most significant publications of the American Jewish community? Who sponsors them and what points of view do they express?

INTO THE MODERN AGE: ZIONISM

Russian Jewry flocked to the Zionist message from its inception. Many of the outstanding "founding fathers" of the movement came from the area of the Pale of Settlement. Dr. Leo Pinsker, Rabbi Zvi Hirsch Kalischer, and Achad Ha'am gave form to the young cause, while Chaim Weizmann, David Ben-Gurion, Moshe Sharett, Levi Eshkol, Golda Meir, and others brought it into being and fruition. Virtually no Jewish movement continues to have such broad support in contemporary Soviet Russia as does Zionism.

Although only founded in Basel in 1897, the Zionist movement met with phenomenal success in the Russian Empire. By the time of the first Russian Zionist Congress in June, 1898, 373 Zionist groups were already in existence.

After the Kishinev pogrom of *Pesach*, 1903, Theodore Herzl travelled to St. Petersburg to meet with high officials of the Tsarist government. During his return, he stopped off in Vilna, Lithuania for the first time. Coincidentally, the first meeting of the Jewish Socialist movement, the Jewish Worker's Union (the Bund) of Russia, Poland, and Lithuania had taken place in 1897 in Vilna. The Bund, as it was called, also aimed at winning the allegiance of the Jewish working masses.

The following is an excerpt from Herzl's diary of August 17, 1903.

> Yesterday, the day of Vilna, will remain engraved in my memory forever.

My arrival at noon in the Russian Polish city was itself the signal for ovations. I have no liking for this sort of thing. On the one side in these receptions is theater—on the other, senseless rapture.

But the business began to be real because it became dangerous when the police, who favored me from the outset with their attentions, forbade any kind of gatherings, and even my visit to the synagogue.

Nevertheless I ended up by driving through tumultuous Jewish streets to the communal offices, where the officials and deputations in packed throngs awaited me. There was a note in their greetings which moved me to a point where nothing but the thought of the newspaper reports was able to restrain my tears.

Address after address praised me wildly beyond what I deserved, but the unhappiness of these sorely oppressed people was only too genuine.

Afterwards various delegations, laden with gifts, called on me at the hotel, in front of which the crowds kept re-gathering as fast as they were dispersed by the police.

... A band of poor youngsters had walked for two hours in order to be able to see me at the table. There they stood, outside, watching my host and I eat and listening to us talk. They finished the dinner music with their Hebrew songs. My host saw that these unbidden guests did not lack for food.

One of these young working-men, in a blue smock, struck me by the hard, determined expression on his face, and I took him to be a revolutionary "Bundist" (Jewish Socialist). To my utter surprise he proposed a toast to the day when "*HaMelech* Herzl" would reign. An absurdity, yet it had an uncanny ring in that dark Russian night.

We drove back, and at one in the morning, from the hotel to the station. The town stayed awake, awaiting my

---

For further background, cf. Baron, pp. 172-181.

departure. The people hurried to the streets through which we passed, lined the roadway, and when they recognized me raised a shout of *Hedad!* From the balconies, too.

The police brutes, who had received instructions to keep the station clear, collided with the crowd. Shouts of *Hedad!* the brutal yell of the police as they hurled themselves at the running crowd, and my driver lashing his horses.

. . . That was Russia.

Questions to Consider

1. Are there any contemporary Jewish figures who would receive a welcome and reception similar to that of Herzl?
2. What did the reception indicate about the strength of Zionist feeling in Russia? How did this feeling develop in the following 20 years, through the period of the revolutions?
3. What were to be the future relations between the Bund and the Zionist movement? What were the solutions tendered by other groups among the Russian Jewish community (Dubnov, Achad Ha'am, etc.)?
4. What was to be the fate of Zionism in Soviet Russia?
5. How would you explain the widespread pro-Zionist feeling in Soviet Russia today, some fifty years after the revolution?
6. What is the condition of Zionist and pro-Israel feeling in contemporary America? Among Jews and non-Jews? Among those identified with synagogues and Jewish schools, and those not affiliated?

THE DECLINE OF TSARIST JEWRY: THE KISHINEV POGROM

With the coming of the 20th century, the Tsarist regime found itself beset within and without by many pressures. Various revolutionary movements, international political events, and a general dissatisfaction with the *status quo* made the need to find some release for these pressures imperative. The regime decided, led by the personal example of Tsar Nicholas II, to aim much of this dissension at the Jews, and thereby to relieve at least the popular feeling against the regime. A series of pogroms was sanctioned, if not sponsored, by the authorities to this end.

The most shocking example of this policy occurred at the height of the Easter holidays, April 19-21, 1903, in the city of Kishinev in the southwest corner of the Russian Empire.

The pogrom evoked worldwide horror. Count Leo Tolstoy, the great Russian author, exclaimed: "I was horrified at the real culprit, namely the government, with its foolish, fanatical priesthood and gang of foolish officials. The Kishinev crime was a consequence of preaching lies and violence, which the government carries on with such stubborn energy. The government's relation to the affair is new proof of its rude egoism, hesitating at no atrocity when it is a question of crushing movements regarded as dangerous. . . ."

Chayim Nachman Bialik, the poet laureate of modern Hebrew literature, wrote an epic poem describing the events at Kishinev. The following is an opening excerpt.

IN THE CITY OF SLAUGHTER

Arise and go now to the city of slaughter;
Into its courtyard wind your way;
There with your hand touch, and with the eyes of your head,
Behold on tree, on stone, on fence, on mural clay,
The spattered blood and dried brains of the dead.
Proceed then to the ruins, the split walls reach,
Where wider grows the hollow, and great grows the breach;
Pass over the shattered hearth, attain the broken wall
Whose burnt and barren brick, whose charred stones reveal
The open mouths of such wounds, that no mending
Shall ever mend, nor healing ever heal.
There will your feet in feathers sink, and stumble
On wreckage doubly wrecked, scroll heaped on manuscript,
Fragments again fragmented—

Pause not upon this havoc; go your way.
The perfumes will be wafted from the acacia bud
And half its blossom will be feathers,
Whose smell is the smell of blood!
And, spiting you, strange incense they will bring—
Banish your loathing—all the beauty of the spring,
The thousand golden arrows of the sun,
Will flash upon your malison;
The sevenfold rays of broken glass
Over your sorrow joyously will pass,
For God called up the slaughter and the spring together—
The slayer slew, the blossom burst, and it was sunny weather!

Then will you flee to a yard, observe its mound.
Upon the mound lie two, and both are headless—
A Jew and his hound.
The self-same axe stuck both, and both were flung
Onto the self-same heap where swine seek dung;

For further background, cf. Baron, pp. 67-70.

*Tomorrow the rain will wash their mingled blood
Into the runnels, and it will be lost
In rubbish heap, in stagnant pool, in mud.
Its cry will not be heard.
It will descend into the deep, or water the cokle-burr.
And all things will be as they ever were....*

Their silence whimpers, and it is their eyes which cry
Wherefore, O Lord, and why?
*It is a silence only God can bear.
Lift then your eyes to the roof; there's nothing there,
Save silences that hang from rafters
And brood upon the air:
Question the spider in his lair!
His eyes beheld these things; and with his web he can
A tale unfold horrific to the ear of man: ...
For these the tales the spider is recounting,
Tales that do puncture the brain, such tales that sever
Your body, spirit, soul, from life, forever!
Then will you bid your spirit*—Hold, enough!
*Stifle the wrath that mounts within your throat,
Bury these things accursed,
Within the depth of your heart, before your heart will burst!
Then will you leave that place, and go your way—
And lo—
The earth is as it was, the sun still shines:
It is a day like any other day.*

*Descend then, to the cellars of the town,
There where the virginal daughters of your folk were fouled,
Where seven heathen flung a woman down,
The daughter in the presence of her mother,
The mother in the presence of her daughter,
Before slaughter, during slaughter, and after slaughter!
Touch with your hand the cushion stained; touch
The pillow incarnadined:*

This is the place the wild ones of the wood, the beasts
  of the field
With bloody axes in their paws compelled your daughters
  yield:
Beasted and swined!
Note also do not fail to note,
In that dark corner, and behind that cask
Crouched husbands, bridegrooms, brothers, peering from
  the cracks,
Watching the sacred bodies struggling underneath
The bestial breath,
Stifled with filth, and swallowing their blood!
Watching from the darkness and its mesh
The lecherous rabble portioning for booty
Their kindred and their flesh!
Crushed in their shame, they saw it all:
They did not stir nor move;
They did not pluck their eyes out, they
Beat not their brains against the wall!
Perhaps, perhaps, each watcher had it in his heart to pray:
A miracle, O Lord—and spare my skin this day! . . .

Questions to Consider

1. Judging by the international reaction, and by the force and power of Bialik's description, how many Jewish lives do you think were lost at Kishinev? How many were in fact killed? What does this indicate about the value of human life some 70 years ago?

2. What poetic ironies of the scene struck Bialik? What ironies have struck you at very dramatic occasions?

3. Elie Wiesel, as the spider in this poem, is a teller of tales. About what kinds of tales does Wiesel write? In what ways are his tales unique?

4. What is Bialik's reaction to the lack of action of the men in the cellars of the town? How would you describe the moral choice these men were confronting? How would you choose what to do?

5. What were the final long range results of the Kishinev pogrom in specific, and this entire Tsarist policy in general?

6. If there were a similar pogrom in America today, how, in your opinion, would this affect American Jewry?

THE DECLINE OF TSARIST JEWRY: THE BEILIS TRIAL

Just prior to World War I, Tsarist Russia had made great strides in entering the modern world. A developing economy based on industrialization, heavy industry, railroads, and mining was expanding into world markets. The creation of the *Duma* (the Russian parliament) modified, at least in theory, the arbitrary powers of the Tsar. Rural organizations were aiding the lot of peasants. However, in the realm of ideology and anti-Semitism, early 20th century Russia had not left the Middle Ages.

The arrest of Mendel Beilis in 1911 on charges of ritually murdering a Christian child shocked the entire civilized world. Nonetheless, the Russian government proceeded to bring the case to trial. Bernard Malamud's *The Fixer* and the film version, succeed in capturing the personal tragedy and conflict felt by the Jewish defendant.

A chief witness for the prosecution, Father Justin Pranaitis, a Catholic priest and author of the pamphlet "The Christians in the Jewish Talmud, or The Secrets of the Teachings of the Rabbis About the Christians" (1893), was called to testify as an expert on Jewish affairs.

The following, from the trial of Mendel Beilis, is a portion of Father Pranaitis' testimony.

> A curse was laid upon the Jewish people by Moses who said: "God will smite you with the botch of Egypt." We see clearly that this curse has been fulfilled, since all European Jews have eczema of the skin, all Asiatic Jews mange upon

their heads, all African Jews boils on their legs, and American Jews a disease of the eyes, as a result of which they are disfigured and stupid. The wicked Rabbis have found a medicinal cure that consists in smearing the afflicted parts with Christian blood.

Their aim in murdering a Christian is threefold: (a) the great hatred they bear the Christians and the assumption that in committing such a murder they are offering a sacrifice to God; (b) the magical actions which they perform with the blood itself; (c) the Rabbis are not certain whether Christ, the son of Mary, was not the real Messiah, and under the circumstances they think they might be saved if they are sprinkled with the said blood.

Four times a year there appears from the air a sort of blood on the Jews' food, and if any Jew tastes of this food he dies. . . . The Rabbis smear a fork with the blood of a martyred Christian and put it on top of their food, so that the blood mentioned above does not fall on their food. . . . When Jews marry, the Rabbis give the bride and bridegroom a boiled egg sprinkled with the ash of a rag that has first been soaked in Christian blood. When the Jews weep over Jerusalem they smear their heads with the above-mentioned ash. At Passover they bake a special dish in which they include the blood of a martyred Christian. When an infant boy is circumcised, the Rabbi takes a beaker of wine into which he puts a drop of blood from the circumcision. When these are well mixed, the Rabbi puts his finger into the beaker and then into the mouth of the infant.

Questions to Consider

1. If you were Beilis' defense attorney, how would you have cross-examined this witness? How would you explain the rituals and customs Father Pranaitis describes?

For further background, cf. Baron, p. 75.

2. How was Tsarist anti-Semitic propaganda different from that of Nazi Germany?

3. Is anti-Semitism still practiced today? In what areas of the world and in what forms? How does contemporary anti-Semitism contrast or compare with historical anti-Semitism?

4. What was the final decision in the trial of Mendel Beilis?

5. Have you ever been totally a victim of circumstances, but unable to free or effectively defend yourself? How did you cope with the situation?

A PRAYER FOR THE TSAR

Notwithstanding the Tsarist regime's policy towards the Jews, prayer on behalf of the royal family was an integral part of every weekly service. It was printed in the *Siddur* of the Tsarist period, placed in the Shabbat liturgy between the *Shacharit* and *Musaf* services.

The following is the prayer as printed in the *Siddur Otzar Hat'fillot* (Vilna, 1914).

PRAYER FOR THE PEACE OF OUR LORD HIS MAJESTY THE TSAR*

May He who gives victory to kings and rule to princes, whose kingdom is eternal; who saved His servant David from the evil sword; He who makes a path in the sea and a way through the strong waves; He should protect, and preserve, and aid, and upraise, and glorify, and carry heavenward our Lord His Majesty the Tsar **NIKOLAI ALEXANDROVITCH** with his revered wife the Tsarina **MARIA FEODOROVNA** with his revered mother the Tsarina **MARIA FEODORVNA** and his son the Crown Prince **ALEXI NIKOLAIEVITCH** and the entire royal family. May the King, the King of Kings, in His mercy extend his life, and protect him, rescue him from all trouble, and sorrow, and harm; and may nations surrender under his feet, and may his enemies fall before him, and to wherever he turns may he meet with success. May the King, the King of Kings, in His mercy place into his heart and in the hearts of all of his advisors and ministers compassion to act kindly with us and with all of Israel. In his days and in ours may Judah be redeemed and Israel dwell in safety, and a redeemer shall come to Zion, and so it may be His will. And let us say: Amen.

The following note is printed in small print in RaSHI script at the bottom of the page, preceded by a reference asterisk:

> *Baruch ben Nariyah wrote from the *Golah* to the inhabitants of Jerusalem telling them to pray for the life of Nebuchadnetzar, the King of Babylonia, and for Belshatzar his son, that they should have as many days as the heavens are over the earth; and Cyrus asked Israel to pray for him (Ezra VI: 10).

Questions to Consider

1. Could the Tsar Nikolai Alexandrovitch (Nicholas II) be considered a friend or an enemy of the Jews?
2. For whom are the Jews praying: only for the Tsar and the royal family, or for someone else as well?
3. Why was the note concerning Nebuchadnetzar and Cyrus added at the bottom of the page? What practical and theological problems does it seek to answer?
4. How could you relate such a prayer to the position taken by Rabbi Shneur Zalman of Lyadi regarding Napoleon some one hundred years earlier?
5. Do you believe that someone should recite a prayer for a country with whose policies he disagrees?
6. After all is said and done, how could the Jews of Tsarist Russia bring themselves to say such a prayer for the Tsar, and even to have it published in their *siddur?* What does

this indicate about a traditional Jewish view of authority, no matter what the regime's policies are?

7. With which policies of the current administration of the United States do many American Jews disagree? How does this affect their loyalty to the United States as a nation?

THE JEWISH POPULATION EXPLOSION

The birthrate of Jews in the United States seems to be lower than that of the general American population. Although no exact statistics are available, it does seem, for example, that most of us do not come from families with a large number of children.

This was not always the case in Jewish life. In the 19th century, the Jewish communities of Eastern Europe and Tsarist Russia experienced a population explosion unparalleled in Jewish history. The extent of the growth rate was such, that this has been termed "the demographic miracle of the Jewish people."

Consider the following three statistical indicators of that phenomenon:

I. *Numbers of Jews and Non-Jews in 19th Century Russia*

Year	Non-Jewish Population	Jewish Population
1820	44,400,000	1,600,000
1851	58,600,000	2,400,000
1880	82,000,000	4,000,000

II. *Gross Increase of Populations*

From 1820 through 1880, the gross increase of the non-Jewish population of Russia was 87%.

From 1820 through 1880, the gross increase of the Jewish population of Russia was 150%.

III. Jewish and Non-Jewish Birth and Mortality Rates

	Birthrate	Infant Mortality Rate
Jews	51.8/1000	15/1000
Non-Jews	51.7/1000	30/1000

Questions to Consider

1. Did the number of Jews decrease, remain the same, or increase from 1820 through 1880, relative to the Russian non-Jewish population? Cite your specific mathematical proof.

2. For every 100 non-Jews in 1820, how many were there in 1880? For every 100 Jews in 1820, how many were there in 1880?

3. How would you account for this Jewish population explosion in 19th century Russia? Were any of these reasons rooted in traditional life and practice?

4. Why is the Jewish rate of increase out of proportion to the non-Jewish population growth?

5. What were the long range effects of this population pool of Russian Jews—for the American Jewish community, for the Jewish settlement in Israel, and for Russian Jewry during the *Shoah* (Holocaust)?

6. In your opinion, is there a specifically Jewish perspective on the current discussion of "Zero Population Growth?" Should Jews support such programs, or not?

7. Within your lifetime, will the number of Jews in the United States and Canada increase or decrease? How many children would you like to have in your own, future family? Why?

For further background, cf. Baron, pp. 76-81.

SOVIET JEWRY UNIT
The Revolution Until the SHOAH

INTRODUCTION

From 1917 through the 1930's the new Soviet government designed and implemented policies which were destined to affect the fate and status of Soviet Jews until the present day. The relation of the Jewish leadership to the State, the place of Hebrew and Yiddish, the status of religious activities, the view of Zionism, and Jewish involvement in the Communist Party and bureaucracy, were all given their initial thrust and direction in that early period.

In this unit we will examine the Russian revolutionary period through the eyes of the editors of a contemporary Hebrew newspaper, *Ha'am*. The vantage point of other Jews will also be considered, including the diaries of Leon Trotsky, and the short stories of Isaac Babel. We will focus on the economic and cultural situation of the Jews, and examine closely how much freedom they were allowed under the new regime.

SOVIET JEWRY: AN OVERVIEW

The following time chart provides a general framework for the Soviet period, both in the general and in the Jewish spheres. Each of the four columns adds a different essential ingredient to the understanding of Soviet Jewish life.

Assignment: In the first two columns ("Changes in Leadership" and "Wars") identify the dates given with specific events and personalities. For the last two columns ("Special Events" and "Jewish Events") be familiar with the significance of the happenings listed. The sequence and especially the correlation of events within a given period should be given special attention. The required information is to be found in a standard history textbook and in Baron.

Changes in Leadership	Wars	Special Events	Jewish Events
	1914-		
1917			1916–*Ha'am* Published
1917			1918–*Yevsektsiya* established
	1918		1919–Pogroms in the Ukraine
	1918-1920		1920
		1921–NEP	
1924			
		1928–Five Year Plan	1928–Birobidzan proposed
			1930–End of *Yevsektsiya*
		1936–Purges	
		1939–Axis Pact	1939–Partition #4 of Poland

1941–1945		1941–*Shoah* begins in USSR
		1945–Red Army captures Berlin
1948–	1948–Berlin	1948–Israel Recognized
	1949–A-Bomb	1948–Arrest of Yiddish Writers
1953	1953–H-Bomb	1953–Doctor's Plot
	1956–Hungary	
	1957–Sputnik	
1958		
1960's		
	1962–Cuba	
1964	1963–Attacks on China Begin	
	1967–50 Years	1967–USSR as Arab Spokesman
	1968–Czech Invasion	1968–Soviet Jewish Protest Movement Begins
		1971–Soviet Government Permits Emigration

Questions to Consider

1. Has the political leadership of the Soviet Union been one of stability or of instability? How might this affect the status of the Jews of the USSR?

2. With which periods do the relations to the Jews seem to take a stricter line?

3. When during these 50 years has the Soviet government encouraged and dealt favorably with its Jews? When has the policy been one of repression? How could you account for these changes?

4. How does the current situation of Soviet Jews compare

with previous periods? Is the Soviet policy today more strict or less strict? How would you account for this?

5. What is your preliminary forecast about the future of Soviet Jewish life in the Soviet Union?

HA'AM

The newspaper *Ha'am* (The People) is a unique historical document. Published in Moscow from November, 1916 through June, 1918, it was the only Hebrew newspaper in Russia spanning the tumultuous periods of the Tsarist, Provisional, and Bolshevik governments. It served as the official organ of the Zionist Party in Moscow, and it supported many national causes of the Jewish people.

"VILNA IN DISTRESS"

This first selection discusses the plight of fellow Jews who were suffering outside of the Russian Empire. With the World War in 1914, the rapid German advances separated many Jews of former Russian-Poland from their brethren and family in the Tsarist Empire. Among these communities was that of Vilna, a major city in Lithuania, and a traditional Jewish center. The ties that bound the Russian Jews to the Jews of Vilna were very strong.

> Fearful rumors reach us from our unfortunate brothers in Vilna.... In truth, the Jerusalem of Lithuania Jewry, the center of Torah and scholarship, never excelled in its material situation. The poverty of Vilna is famous throughout world Jewry. Her citizens would always manage with little and would never appeal for outside help ... Therefore, when Vilna turns for aid, if aristocratic Vilna cries in public, it is a sign that she has no choice....

Questions to Consider

1. Because of what virtue was Vilna termed "aristocratic" and "the Jerusalem of Lithuania?"
2. For what kinds of Jewish activities was Vilna famous?
3. What was the Jewish population of Vilna at the turn of the 20th century? How would you compare the image of Vilna at the time of Herzl's visit in 1903, with the situation described in this editorial?
4. What remains of "Jewish" Vilna today?
5. How many Jewish poor are there in America today? How are they being cared for? What is our responsibility towards them?

"THE ELECTION CAMPAIGN"

January 7-9, 1918 marked the elections for the All-Russian Jewish Congress, a body which, it was hoped, would serve as the future national organization for Russian Jewry. The delegates to the Congress were to be elected by a vote of all of the Russian Jews. The competing parties for the votes of this Jewish electorate included the Zionists and the Bundists (the Jewish Socialists).

The Bund launched a particularly vociferous campaign. They did not want the victory of the "reactionary Jewish nationalists" as they called the Zionists, and took various measures in an attempt to defeat them. In the end, however, the Zionists won a resounding victory, capturing 62 delegates to only 21 for the Bund.

For further background, cf. Baron, pp. 187-195, 274.

The following editorial by the editor-in-chief of *Ha'am* Dr. Moshe Glikson, is a post-election evaluation of the campaign waged by the Bund.

> At this time (of the elections) the few remnants of the carriers of the flag of national heresy do fierce battle with the living will and the work of the nation coming to rebirth. To this we would have no objection. We can understand their sorrow born out of downfall and defeat.
>
> However, they do not suffice with battle alone, but they also contaminate our world and poison the public air around us. They blame Judaism with crude accusations, designed not only to degrade our name, but also to expose Jews in various towns to real danger. It is impossible to read with lack of emotion the deep bitterness with which the Bund "literature" was publicized during the last elections. One example will suffice.
>
> In Moscow the Bundists plastered the walls and streets with tens of thousands of posters, on each fence and wall, and especially in the Russian language, the language known to the rabble, who are waiting around the market and the streets these days, and who are willing and able at any time to show its fist to the bourgeoise and to the other "enemies of the people." And these posters are signed in the name of "The Russian Social Democratic (Bolshevik) Party," capped with the well known slogan "Workers of the World—Unite!", and state that the greatest and most dangerous enemy to democracy and the masses, not to the Jewish democracy or the Jewish masses, but to the democracy and masses alone, are the Zionists. These are "our worse enemies"; "they are the ones who want annexation and conquests, and are trying to lengthen the war. . . ."

For further background, cf. Baron, pp. 168-181, 201-209.

Questions to Consider

1. What was the Bund? When and where was it founded? How did it differ from the Zionist Party in its goals and platform? What was its relation to Lenin's Bolshevik Party?
2. Outline the tactics used by the Bund in the election campaign.
3. What do the tactics of the Bund indicate about the nature of the struggle for the control of the Jewish masses after the Bolshevik Revolution?
4. What future Jewish organization in Soviet Russia do the Bund's tactics anticipate?
5. Assuming that the Bund's contentions were justified, how do you react to their tactics?
6. In what kind of political situations do the ends justify the means, if ever?
7. Are there any cases of Jews publicly attacking other Jewish causes? In your opinion, is this proper or not?

"THE SEPARATION OF CHURCH AND STATE"

The Bolshevik Revolution in November, 1917 held out great hopes to the Russian people, and to the Jews no less than anyone else. After holding second-class status from the Tsarist authorities, the Jewish leadership hoped that the new government would support a multitude of Jewish causes and activities. The decrees which separated church from state of February, 1918 came as a great shock to the Jewish leadership and masses. Dr. Moshe Glikson, the editor of *Ha'am*, voiced the following concern: "There is a fear that the new decree will be like the edicts of Antiochus, and whoever wishes to teach his son Torah or the Hebrew language will have to go into hiding for fear of persecution by the new authority."

DECREE OF THE SOVIET OF PEOPLE'S COMMISSARS ON THE SEPARATION OF CHURCH FROM STATE AND SCHOOL FROM CHURCH, FEBRUARY 5, 1918

1. The Church is separated from the state.
2. Within the boundaries of the Republic it is forbidden to publish any local laws or decisions which would obstruct or limit freedom of conscience or would establish any advantages or privileges based on the religious faith to which the citizen belongs.
3. Every citizen may profess any religion or none. All disabilities connected with the profession of any faith or with the non-profession of any are abolished.
4. Acts of state and other public official functions are not to be accompanied by any religious rites or ceremonies.
5. Free practice of religious rites is guaranteed in so far as this does not violate public order and is not accompanied by attacks on the rights of citizens of the Soviet Republic.
6. No one may decline to carry out his civil obligations on account of his religious views. Exceptions to this rule are permitted in each individual case by virtue of a decision of the People's Court.
8. Civil acts are under the exclusive control of the civil government: the departments of registration of marriages and births.
9. The school is separated from the Church.

Religious teaching is not permitted in any state, public, or private institution of learning where general educational subjects are taught.

Citizens may teach and study religion privately.

10. All church and religious societies are not to receive

any privileges or subsidies from the state or local institutions.

11. Compulsory taxes or collections for church or religious societies are not permitted.

12. No church or religious societies possess the right to own property. They do not possess the right of a juridical person.

13. All the possessions of the church and religious societies existing in Russia are declared the property of the people.

Buildings and objects which are especially designed for the purposes of service are handed over by special decisions of the central and local governmental authorities for the free use of the appropriate religious societies.

President of the Soviet of People's Commissars:
V. ULIANOV (LENIN)

Questions to Consider

1. What was the position and power of the Church establishment in Tsarist Russia?

2. What rights did synagogues have in Russia prior to the Bolshevik revolution? What rights did the synagogue have under this new legislation?

3. What is allowed under the new law? What is forbidden?

4. How does the concept of "the separation of church and state" differ in the Soviet Union and in the United States?

5. What would the consequences be for the American Jewish community if such a law were passed by the United States Congress? What present practices would then be forbidden?

6. Were Dr. Glikson's fears substantiated after 1918? How does the situation regarding Jewish communal organization, activity, and education in Soviet Russia today compare with his prediction of more than 50 years ago?

"THE REVOLUTION"

Writing just after the November Bolshevik Revolution, the founder and chief political analyst of *Ha'am*, Bentzion Katz, indicates in what directions he sees the revolution headed. His sharpness and courage are qualities which were as rare then as they are today. Katz continued to write signed editorials objecting to the tactics and policies of the new regime. *Ha'am* finally closed in the spring of 1918, when its major financial backers fled Bolshevik Russia to the Ukraine.

> The Russian "Revolution" in her excesses rises much above the negative visions of revolutionary France. The Bolsheviks have done things which remind us not of the French Revolution but of primitive pogroms in the Russian style.
>
> Even Nicholas' ministers would not have dared to act as coarsely to the Duma as these "extreme socialists" (the Bolsheviks) relate to the Constituent Assembly.
>
> Difficult days are still awaiting the state. If they do not allow the Constituent Assembly to meet, anarchy will grow in the state, and who knows what the future days will bring.
>
> In reality, our only hope is that the new inquisitionary government will not last long.
>
> B.K.

Questions to Consider

1. To what "excesses" was Katz referring?
2. What, in fact, was the fate of the Constituent Assembly?
3. Which of the following descriptive terms would you

associate primarily with the Tsarist regime, and which would you associate primarily with the Bolshevik regime? Why?

bloody	repressive
bureaucratic	centralistic
ruthless	democratic
corrupt	progressive
anti-Semitic	backward
against anti-Semitism	aristocratic
against Judaism	common
not against Judaism	romantic
pro-United States	revolutionary
anti-United States	Jewish

JEWS IN THE COMMUNIST PARTY

Although the Jews constituted only 3-5% of the total population of the Soviet State, the number of Jews who belonged to the Soviet Communist Party in the early years of the revolution was far greater. At the highest level, half of the members of the ruling first Politbureau were Jews. A likewise large proportion of Jews filtered down into the ranks of the Party. This led opponents of the Soviet regime to use anti-Semitism as one very effective method of combating the newly established Soviet government. The "White Army" forces opposing Soviet rule in the Ukraine perpetrated many pogroms against the local Jewish population, in the period of the 1919-1920 Civil War. There were Jews who initially supported the Bolshevik regime because the Red Army was the only armed force which would protect the Jews from the pogromists. Others joined the Communists on principle, believing that a new era was beginning for the Jewish people and for mankind.

In spite of the large number of Jewish Communists, most of the Jews in the leadership ranks of the Party were totally removed from any committed Jewish life or associations. In fact, the Soviet government chose to establish an entirely separate unit to deal specifically with the Yiddish-speaking Jewish nationality in the Soviet Union, the Jewish Sections of the Communist Party (*Yevsektsiya*).

The following is a partial list of Jews in the Communist Party who attained notable rank or distinction. For further

THE REVOLUTION UNTIL THE *SHOAH* 83

biographical information consult the *Encyclopedia of Russia and the Soviet Union* by Michael Florinsky (McGraw-Hill Co., New York City, 1961) and the *Encyclopedia Judaica* (Keter Publishing House Limited, Jerusalem, 1971).

Name (or Pseudonym)	Title or Function
Simon Dimanstein	Head of National Minorities Department, Central Committee, Communist Party of the Soviet Union.
Yan Gamarnik	First Secretary, Belorussian Communist Party. Head of Political Administration of Red Army.
Lazar Kaganovich	Chairman of Communist Party Control Commission. First Deputy Minister of USSR Council of Ministers.
Lev Rosenfeld (Lev Kamenev)	First Chairman of the Central Executive Committee of the Soviets.
Mikhiel Lurye (Yu. Larin)	Leading Communist Economist who Authorized Nationalization Program.
Maxim Wallach (Maxim Litvinov)	Commissar of Foreign Affairs for the USSR in the 1930's.
Solomon Dridzo (Solomon Lozovsky)	Secretary-General of Red International of Labor (Profintern).
Karl Sobelsohn (Karl Radek)	Secretary of the Communist International. Chief Soviet Propagandist.
Grigory Brilliant (Grigory Sokolnikov)	People's Commissar of Finance. Ambassador of the USSR to Great Britain.
Yakov Sverdlov	Chairman of the Central Executive Committee of the Congress of Soviets. Secretary, Central Committee of the Bolshevik Party.
Lev Bronstein (Leon Trotsky)	War Commissar. Leader of the Red Army.
Yona Yakir	General in the Red Army. Leader of the Ukrainian Communist Party.

Name (or Pseudonym)	Title or Function
Yemelyan Gubelman (Yemelyan Yaroslavsky)	President, League of Militant Atheists.
Jacob Yurovsky	Red Army Officer in Charge of Executing Tsar Nicholas II and the Royal Family.
Grigory Radomyslsky (Grigory Zinoviev)	Chairman, Executive Committee of the Communist International (Comintern).

Questions to Consider

1. In which areas of public life were Jews active in the revolutionary and post-revolutionary periods of Soviet history?

2. What does the various positions these people held indicate about the place of Jews in the Communist Party and in Russia during this period?

3. How does this compare with the current status of Jews in the leadership of the Soviet Union? When did the change in status occur?

4. Why did the Jews come to occupy such important positions within the Communist Party and State hierarchies? Why were there relatively so many Russian Jews who were active as revolutionaries?

5. If you were to make a similar listing of leading American Jewish political, military, and national leaders, whom would you include? Would their positions and rank be comparable with those attained by Jews in the Communist Party and Soviet government? How would you account for this disparity?

6. Why are there relatively so many American Jews who are active in non-establishment causes?

LEON TROTSKY AND THE JEWS

Lev Davidovich Bronstein, the son of a Ukrainian Jewish farmer, played a unique and critical role in modern Russian revolutionary history. Under the pseudonym Trotsky he rose to leadership as chairman of the Petrograd Soviet, head of the Military Revolutionary Committee, and Commissar for War of the Red Army. He was second only to Lenin himself. At the time of Lenin's death in 1924, Stalin defeated Trotsky in a Kremlin power play, and Trotsky was exiled. Finding his way to Mexico City, in 1940 he was assassinated by a secret agent of Stalin's police.

It is only possible to speculate as to what the future would have held for Soviet Jews had Trotsky taken over as head of the Soviet state. However, some interesting historical parallels do present themselves. Other Jews (or non-Jews with Jewish wives) have served as heads of governments in the modern age, as Leon Blum in France, and Wadaslaw Gomulka in Poland. How has their being Jewish (or their wives' Jewishness) affected their positions? Has this fact been used against them, aided them, or been ignored? What would happen if a Jew were elected President of the United States? How, in your opinion, would this affect his domestic and foreign policies, if at all?

The following selections were written by Trotsky in 1937 in exile. In his continuing polemic against Stalin, he discussed the continued existence of anti-Semitism in Soviet Russia.

> It has not been forgotten, I trust, that anti-Semitism was quite widespread in Tsarist Russia, among the peasant, the

petty bourgeois of the city, the intelligentsia, and the more backward strata of the working class. "Mother" Russia was renowned not only for her periodic Jewish pogroms but also for the existence of a considerable number of anti-Semitic publications which, in that day, enjoyed a wide circulation. The October revolution abolished the outlawed status against the Jews. That, however, does not mean at all that with one blow it swept out anti-Semitism. A long and persistent struggle against religion has failed to prevent suppliants even today from crowding thousands and thousands of churches, mosques and synagogues. The same situation prevails in the sphere of national prejudices. Legislation alone does not change people. Their thoughts, emotions, outlook depend upon tradition, material conditions of life, cultural level, etc. The Soviet regime is not yet twenty years old. The older half of the population was educated under Tsarism. The younger half has inherited a great deal from the older.

But this is by no means all. The Soviet regime, in actuality, initiated a series of new phenomena which, because of the poverty and low cultural level of the population, were capable of generating anew, and did in fact generate, anti-Semitic moods. The Jews are typical city population. They comprise a considerable percentage of the city population in the Ukraine, in White Russia, and even in Great Russia. The Soviet, more than any other regime in the world, needs a very great number of civil servants. Civil servants are recruited from the more cultured city population. Naturally the Jews occupied a disproportionately large place among the bureaucracy and particularly so in its lower and middle levels. Of course we can close our eyes to that fact and limit ourselves to vague generalities about the equality and brotherhood of all races. But an ostrich policy will not advance us a single step. *The hatred of the peasants and the workers for the bureaucracy is a fundamental fact in Soviet life* (italics Trotsky's). . . . It is impossible not to conclude that the hatred for the bureaucracy would assume an anti-Semitic color, at least in those places where the Jewish functionaries compose a significant percentage of the population and are thrown into relief against the broad background of the peasant masses. . . . The antagonism between the population and the bureaucracy has grown monstrously during the past ten to twelve years. All serious and honest observers, especially those who have lived among the toiling masses for a long time, bear witness to the existence of anti-Semitism, not only of the old and hereditary, but also of the new, "Soviet" variety.

. . . Some would-be "pundits" have even accused me of "suddenly" raising the "Jewish question" and of intending to create some kind of ghetto for the Jews. I can only shrug my shoulders in pity. I have lived my whole life outside of Jewish circles. I have always worked in the Russian worker's movement. My native tongue is Russian. Unfortunately, I have not even learned to read Jewish. The Jewish question therefore has never occupied the center of my attention. But that does not mean that I have the right to be blind to the Jewish problem which exists and demands solution.

Questions to Consider

1. What is Trotsky's approach to Tsarist and recent Soviet history? How does his approach to history differ from a presentation by a more "establishment" Soviet historian?

2. What two reasons does he give for the continuation of anti-Semitism in the Soviet Union? Are these reasons still operative today?

3. What new factors have been added since Trotsky's time which might serve to intensify the anti-Semitic feeling in Soviet Russia?

4. In 1918, the Soviet People's Commissars published a

decree entitled "Concerning the Suppression of the Roots of the Anti-Semitic Movement," discouraging pogroms and all other anti-Semitic behavior. Lenin himself made a recording attacking anti-Semitism. Why was the early Soviet government so much opposed to pogroms and anti-Semitism? Is the contemporary Soviet government anti-Semitic? Discuss.

5. Which professions of United States' Jewry throw us "into relief against the broad background of the peasant masses?" How has this effected the status of U.S. Jews, and the growth of anti-Semitism in America?

6. How would you speculate as to the future of Soviet Jewry if Trotsky had taken control of the Soviet state?

For further background, cf. Baron, pp. 203-204.

THE *YEVSEKTSIYA*

Not all the Jews of revolutionary Russia were as favorably disposed to their brethren as were *Ha'am* and Trotsky. A large cadre of militant anti-religious, anti-clerical, and anti-Zionist Jews was also grouping itself. The Jewish Sections of the Communist Part (the *Yevsektsiya*) began their work in the first few months after the revolution.

Their major functions were to destroy the old order, to bring Communism to the Jewish masses, and to reorder and rebuild Jewish life and the war ravaged Jewish economic situation. The *Yevsektsiya's* attack on the traditional Jewish way of life was particularly unrelenting. Propaganda and scorn were the main instruments invoked. Public show trials were conducted of religious customs and institutions. Among other anti-religious acts, the "Jewish religion" was put on trial in Kiev in 1921, a *"Yeshivah"* was tried in Rostov, and "Circumcision" in Kharkov in 1928. All were, of course, found "guilty." All of these activities were conducted almost exclusively by Jews against other Jews.

From 1921 onwards, the *Yevsektsiya* was the only legal organization allowed to function within the Jewish community. Formal religious instruction for persons under the age of 18 was made illegal, although private religious education between parent and child was permitted. By 1929-1930 nearly 650 synagogues had been converted by the *Yevsektsiya* into social halls and worker's clubs. One of the major targets of the *Yevsektsiya* was the Zionist Movement and organization.

The following resolution was adopted by the Second Conference of the Jewish Communist Sections in Moscow, in June, 1919:

> The Zionist party plays a counter-revolutionary role, and is responsible for strengthening among the backward Jewish masses the influence of clericalism and nationalist attitudes. In this way the class self-determination of the Jewish toiling masses is undermined and the penetration of Communist ideas in their midst seriously hindered. Owing to its Palestine policy, the Zionist party serves as an instrument of united imperialism which combats the proletarian revolution. In consideration of all these circumstances, the Conference requests the Central Bureau to propose the pertinent authorities the promulgation of a decree suspending all activities of the Zionist party, in the economic, political, and cultural spheres. The communal organs, which are the mainstay of all reactionary forces within the Jewish people, must be suppressed.

For further background, cf. Baron, pp. 208-214.

Questions to Consider

1. For what specific crimes is the Zionist party singled out? How else did the *Yevsektsiya* seek to defeat these specific "enemies of the revolution?"

2. What action is the *Yevsektsiya* recommending to the Party Central Committee?

3. Was this policy of the *Yevsektsiya* and the Soviet government regarding Zionism successful? What remains of the Zionist movement and Zionist feeling in contemporary Soviet Russia? How would you explain this?

4. What does this document suggest about the position and strength of the Zionist party in post-revolutionary Russia?

5. In spite of this statement in 1919, the Soviet policy regarding Palestine and Israel has gone through a number of stages. When has the Soviet policy been decidedly anti-Israel and how has the Soviet government implemented this policy? When has the Soviet policy been decidedly pro-Israel and how has the Soviet government implemented this policy?

6. What was the final fate of the *Yevsektsiya* and of most of its leadership?

7. Have there been other Jews or Jewish groups which have publicly come out as anti-Zionist or anti-Israel? How would you answer their allegations?

ISAAC BABEL

Isaac Babel (1894-1940?) was one of the foremost short story writers of modern Russian literature. He has been compared with such Russian greats as Chekov and Tolstoy. With the advent of recent translations of his works into English, he has become known to American audiences as well.

Born the son of a Jewish shopkeeper in Odessa, Babel was exposed to a traditional Jewish education of Hebrew, Bible, and Talmud until the age of sixteen. Joining the Communist party at an early age, he served during the Civil War on the Polish and Ukrainian fronts. He was assigned to a Cossack brigade as a Communist Party worker. His book of short stories *Red Cavalry* describes the war as seen through his definitely Bolshevik, yet profoundly Jewish, eyes. Few modern Jewish writers have succeeded in capturing the tensions and interaction between the Jewish and outside worlds as does Babel in his writing.

Read for pleasure and then study carefully the following story.

THE RABBI'S SON

Do you remember Zhitomir, Vasily? Do you remember the River Teterev, Vasily, and that night when the Sabbath, the young Sabbath crept along the sunset, crushing the stars beneath her little red heel?

The slender horn of the moon bathed its darts in the dark waters of the river. Queer old Gedali, the founder of the Fourth International, led us to Rabbi Motale Bratslavsky's for evening prayers. Queer old Gedali shook the cock's feathers on his top hat in the ruddy haze of evening. The predatory eyes of lighted candles blinked in the Rabbi's room. Broad-shouldered Jews groaned dully, bent over prayerbooks, and the old buffoon of the Chernobyl saddiks jingled coppers in his frayed pocket.

Do you remember that night, Vasily? Beyond the window, horses were neighing and Cossacks shouted. The wilderness of war yawned beyond the window, and Rabbi Motale Bratslavsky prayed by the eastern wall, digging his emaciated fingers into his talith. Then the curtain of the Ark was drawn aside, and we saw in the funeral candlelight the Torah rolls sheathed in covers of purple velvet and blue silk and, bowed above the Torah, inanimate and resigned, the beautiful face of Elijah the Rabbi's son, last prince of the dynasty.

Well, only the day before yesterday, Vasily, the regiments of the XII Army opened the front at Kovel. The conqueror's bombardment thundered disdainfully over the town. Our troops faltered, and mingled in confusion. The Political Section train started crawling over the dead backbone of the fields. And a monstrous and inconceivable Russia tramped in bast shoes on either side of coaches, like a multitude of bugs swarming in clothes. The typhus-ridden peasantry rolled before them the customary humpback of a soldier's death. They jumped up on to the steps of our train and fell back, dislodged by the butt-ends of our rifles. They snorted and scrabbled and flowed on wordlessly. And at the twelfth verst, when I had no potatoes left, I flung a pile of Trotsky's leaflets at them. But only one man among them stretched a dead and filthy hand to catch a leaflet. And I recognized Elijah, son of the Rabbi of Zhitomir. I recognized him at once, Vasily. And it was so heartrending to see a prince who had lost his pants, doubled up beneath his soldier's pack, that we defied the regulations and pulled him up into our coach. His bare knees, inefficient as an old woman's, knocked against the rusty iron of the steps. Two full-bosomed typists in sailor blouses trailed the long, shamed body of the dying man along the floor. We laid him in a corner of the editorial office, on the floor, and Cossacks in loose red trousers set straight the clothes that were dropping off him. The girls planted their bandy legs—legs of unforward females—on the floor, and stared dully at his sexual organs, the stunted, curly-covered virility of a wasted Semite. And I, who had seen him on one of my nights of roaming, began to pack in a case the scattered belongings of the Red Army man Bratslavsky.

His things were strewn about pell-mell—mandates of the propagandist and notebooks of the Jewish poet, the portraits of Lenin and Maimonides lay side by side, the knotted iron of Lenin's skull beside the dull silk of the portraits of Maimonides. A lock of woman's hair lay in a book, the Resolutions of the Party's Sixth Congress, and the margins of Communist leaflets were crowded with crooked lines of ancient Hebrew verse. They fell upon me in a mean and depressing rain—pages of the Song of Songs and revolver cartridges. The dreary rain of sunset washed the dust in my hair, and I said to the boy who was dying on a wretched mattress in the corner:

"One Friday evening four months ago, Gedali the old-clothesman took me to see your father, Rabbi Motale. But you didn't belong to the Party at that time, Bratslavsky . . ."

"I did," the boy answered, scratching at his chest and twisting in fever, "only I couldn't leave my mother."

"And now, Elijah?"

"When there's a revolution on, a mother's an episode," he whispered, less and less audibly. "My letter came, the letter B, and the Organization sent me to the front. . . ."

"And you got to Kovel, Elijah?"

"I got to Kovel!" he cried in despair. "The kulaks opened the front to the enemy. I took over the command of a scratch regiment, but too late . . . I hadn't enough artillery. . . ."

He died before we reacher Rovno. He—that last of the Princes—died among his poverty, phylacteries, and coarse foot-wrappings. We buried him at some forgotten station. And I, who can scarce contain the tempests of my imagination within this age-old body of mine, I was there beside my brother when he breathed his last.

Questions to Consider

1. What Jewish references does Babel include in the story? In what ways does he express his familiarity with Jewish life and experiences?

2. Babel describes the conflict between the revolution and Judaism on a very personal level. How does Babel come to grips with, or attempt to solve, this conflict?

3. How would you translate this underlying theme of Babel's into your own life and experience? Into the experience of the Jewish people throughout history? How do you resolve for yourself this conflict? How did the Jewish people resolve the conflict?

For further background, cf. Baron, pp. 287-289. Other stories which will be of particular interest include: "The Cemetery at Kozin" and "The Rabbi" in *The Collected Stories* (Meridian Books, World Publishing Co., New York—$1.95). "Shabos Nahamu" and "The Jewess" in *You Must Know Everything* by Natalie Babel (Farrar, Straus and Giroux, New York —$5.95, and other publishers).

THE SOVIET JEWISH ECONOMY

Economics play a vital role in the Soviet conception of society and its organization. The major thrust of virtually every Communist revolution is to redistribute the means of production and the earning powers of the population. The state takes over the control and the running of many formerly private enterprises, a massive civil service absorbs into its ranks a large bureaucracy, and private businessmen are eliminated.

Among the most serious results of the revolution for the Jews of Russia was the undermining of their traditional place as middleman in the Russian economy. Jews had been involved in all facets of the Tsarist economy, including banking, insurance companies, textiles, sea transport, as well as sugar, coal, oil, and gold production and mining. They served both as the employers and the workers. Many, of course, were businessmen, artisans, and peddlers. Many found themselves placed in an impossible economic position, and the massive readjustment took a great toll.

The following chart presents the distribution of the occupations of the Russian Jews (in percentages) according to different years.

Occupation	1913	1934	1939
clerks	7%	33. %	37.2%
free professions	3%	7.8%	12.8%
workers	20%	23.6%	21.5%
farmers	2%	8.7%	7.1%
artisans	27%	16. %	14.3%
businessmen	29%	2.5%	—
miscellaneous	12%	7.8%	7.1%

For further background, cf. Baron, pp. 249-267.

96 JEWS IN RUSSIA: LAST FOUR CENTURIES

Questions to Consider

1. How would you characterize the economic changes in Russian Jewry with the Bolshevik revolution?
2. What had been the major occupation of Russian Jews before the revolution? Why had it dropped so drastically?
3. Which new occupations had shown the greatest rise with the revolution? Do these new occupations require relatively more or less education, and more or less urbanization? What does this indicate about other changes in the Soviet Jewish population.
4. If you were a Ukrainian peasant in 1913, and were shown the first column on the chart, how would you interpret it? Would this tend to make you more philo- or anti-Semitic?
5. If you were this same Ukrainian peasant, turned factory worker in 1939, and were shown the entire chart, how would you interpret it? How would you view the contemporary contribution of Soviet Jews to general Soviet society? Would this tend to make you more philo- or anti-Semitic?
6. How does the occupational division and distribution of the occupations of the Jews of the United States affect the image the non-Jews have of us?
7. What would happen to your father's job and security if capitalism in the United States were ever to be replaced by a communist system?

SOVIET JEWISH BOOK PUBLISHING

One of the clearest indicators of the pulse and spirit of American society is to examine the "best seller" book lists. Current concerns, pleasures, and interests are often very clearly suggested. Those who have visited a major Jewish bookstore know how true this is in microcosm. Especially since the Jewish people have been so literarily inclined, whether in sacred texts or in popular works, has this area of expression been so important.

Although surprising to many, from the Bolshevik revolution until the *Shoah*, Soviet Russia was the undisputed Yiddish publishing center of the world. No other country even approached the number and mass circulation of the State sponsored Yiddish publishing houses.

The following statistics reveal the massiveness of the Soviet publishing endeavor.

Year	Number of Yiddish Books and Pamphlets	Yiddish Newspapers
1917	150	49
1918	237	63
1919	274	58
1920	106	96
1921	85	62
1922	68	27
1923	40	21
1924	76	21
1925	168	21
1926	164	26
1927	217	40

1928	238	?
1929	319	?
1930	531	?
1931	496	?
1932	668	?
1933	391	?
1934	348	?
1935	437	41
1936	431	?
1937	356	?
1938	348	?
1939	339	?
1940	359	?
June/1941	202	13
	7,048	538

For further background, cf. Baron, pp. 278-287.

Questions to Consider

1. Why did the Soviet government in this pre-war period encourage such an extensive Yiddish press and publication network?

2. What do these statistics indicate about the Jewish nationality policy of the Soviet Union in this period?

3. Often, Soviet government spokesmen will cite these and similar publishing figures to "prove" the freedom Soviet Jews enjoy. What additional and more detailed information would you have to know in order to substantiate or disprove this claim?

4. How is Soviet press and publication different from American press and publication?

5. What is the extent of censorship in the Soviet press? What was the censorship policy of the Tsarist government?

What is the extent of censorship in the American press and publishing field?

The following is a detailed breakdown of the 437 Yiddish books published in the Soviet Union in 1935, by subject matter.

I.	Marxism-Leninism	14
II.	Communist Party	22
III.	Political Science	17
IV.	Economics	12
V.	Belles Lettres	201
VI.	Educational Texts	54
VII.	Children's Books	83
VIII.	Arts and Technical Books	23
IX.	Miscellaneous	11

Questions to Consider

1. Which were the major categories of Yiddish books published in 1935?

2. Which categories of books were *not* published in the Soviet Union that year?

3. What does this indicate about the Jewish nationality policy of the Soviet government, and especially of the use of the Yiddish language?

PUBLISHING IN THE HEBREW LANGUAGE

In addition to the thousands of Yiddish books published in the Soviet Union from the Revolution until 1960, some 250 have been published in Hebrew, and 148 in the Russian language on Jewish themes.

The following is a breakdown of the number of publications in the Soviet Union in Hebrew, by subject matter, and with dates of publication.

Subjects		Total Published	Publishing Information
I.	Religious Books (32 *Sidurim,* 22 calendars, 21 *Tanach* and Rabbinics)	75	71 until 1929, 1 *Siddur* in 1957, calendars in 1956, 1957, 1959.
II.	Zionism	13	all until 1919.
III.	History and Philosophy	12	11 until 1919, 1 in 1920.
IV.	Dictionary and Literary Criticism	11	all until 1919.
V.	Belles Letters	28	26 until 1919, 1 in 1923, 1 in 1927.
VI.	Children's Books	55	all until 1919.
VII.	Text Books	22	20 until 1919, 2 in 1920
VIII.	Newspapers and Periodicals	35	31 until 1919, 1 each in 1920, 1923, 1926, 1928.

For further background, cf. Baron, pp. 273-278.

Questions to Consider

1. What was the extent of Hebrew-language culture and life in Tsarist Russia? What was the fate of the Hebrew language in Soviet Russia?

2. How would you compare subjects of books published in Hebrew with the subjects of those published in Yiddish (consider the figures given for Yiddish publishing in 1935 as a representative year)?

3. Until what period did most of the Hebrew publishing in the Soviet Union flourish? How would you account for the demise of Hebrew publishing in the Soviet Union?

4. How does a comparison of the quantity and types of Yiddish and Hebrew publishing help to explain the Soviet nationality policy regarding the Jews?

5. Why did the Soviet government draw such a distinction between the use of Hebrew and Yiddish? In what other realms was this distinction between Hebrew and other languages also expressed?

6. How has Hebrew replaced Yiddish in popularity and use in the United States? Is there a future for any language other than English in the United States as the language of Jewish youth and intellectuals?

THE PRE-*SHOAH* SOVIET JEW

With the economic readjustment after the revolution, Soviet Jews became more urbanized, better educated, and increasingly members of the ruling Soviet bureaucracy and establishment. A serious attempt was made to integrate the Jews into many aspects of Soviet society. The work of the *Yevsektsiya* in the 1920's in closing down various synagogues and in militating against religious practices had set the tone for the period. In addition, the purges of the 1930's brought the closing of Yiddish schools, the elimination of much of a Jewish presence in the ranks of the Communist Party, and a general stifling of non-Party thought and behavior.

These factors brought about a desire on the part of many Soviet Jews to assimilate.

However, the events of the late 1930's signalled a radical change in this process. The Fourth Partition of Poland in 1939 brought into the Soviet Union some 2,000,000 actively identified Jews from Estonia, Latvia, Lithuania, and eastern Poland. They had been part of a live and vibrant Jewish culture.

The following eyewitness account brings out most forcefully the contrast between the Sovietized Jew of Russia, and the Jews of the formerly independent states of the Baltic region and Poland.

> During Passover, 1940, I had an opportunity of talking to the Soviet Commander D., a Jew from Homel in White Russia. He was an officer in the Red Army Artillery, and on Passover Eve he came to the synagogue in order to see, as

he put it, "What is going on in this brightly illuminated building."

He was astonished when I told him that this was the Eve of Passover and that Jews had gathered to pray and celebrate the Festival of Liberation. He said: "For the past twenty years I haven't even known when this festival occurs. Among us only the handful of surviving old folk permit themselves to pray, and they pray in a corner so that nobody may notice. But the young people haven't the slightest idea of these out-dated customs and aren't interested in them." The adult Jews, like himself, still remember how they asked father the Questions when they were children. "But, he added, "now nobody asks questions among us. . . ."

I invited him to be my guest for the Seder. He accepted the invitation and came to our home. At the beginning of the Seder he behaved rather casually, but when it came to "Pour forth thy wrath upon the gentiles" a sigh burst forth from his lips and with tears in his eyes he said: 'How pleasant this is! But what a pity that because of our many sins we are forbidden to celebrate our festivals and have our children know these beautiful customs and festivals! The younger generation that will take our place will not even know that there is a Jewish religion with meaningful festivals."

Before he left he stood up and said the "Shehechiyanu," the blessing for having lived to experience this occasion. He thanked us for inviting him, and pressing my hand he said: "After this Seder I am capable of living decades longer, if it is to be my fate, among gentiles. And I shall not forget the time and the meaning of 'Pour forth thy wrath,' and maybe I shall even be able to teach something of this to my children."

The officer left. In the room there was a deep shadow. The electric light seemed to grow dim in the shadow of this huge Jewish community beyond reach and without content or tradition in their lives. And perhaps it was because we felt that we were about to go through the same process, and that this might be our last Seder during these dreadful years.

Questions to Consider

1. What had Jewish life been like in interbellum (between the two World Wars) Poland and the Baltic states? How did it differ or compare with the development of Jewish life in Soviet Russia in the same period?

2. Why was the Red Army officer so touched and affected by the experience?

3. The officer said that this *Pesach* would sustain him for many years after the experience. What personal experiences have you had which sustained you for a long period afterwards?

4. Did the prophecy of the officer regarding the younger generation come to fulfillment? Why or why not?

5. In what ways is contemporary Jewish life in the Baltic regions different from that of the Russian and Ukrainian Republics? How does Jewish life in Soviet Georgia and Central Asia differ from the rest of the USSR?

SOVIET JEWRY UNIT
The Shoah

INTRODUCTION

The effects of the *Shoah* (the Holocaust) are still being felt in our contemporary Jewish world. With a pre-*Shoah* population of over 16,000,000, today the world Jewish population barely reaches 14,250,000. In addition to the demographic decrease, the loss in terms of Jewish scholarship, leadership, and "Jewish souls" was catastrophic.

In this unit we will examine the process of extermination as it was framed and implemented in Soviet Russia, and various forms of resistance to the Nazis. Our travels will extend from the Polish death camp Maidanek and the offices of the British Broadcasting Corporation in London, to the Jewish Anti-Fascist Committee in Moscow.

It is important to recall that the western borders of the Soviet Union went through various changes and modifications during the War. In January, 1939, the Jewish population of the USSR numbered 3,000,000. With the territorial annexations of 1939-1940, the total rose to 5,000,000, including Jews from former parts of Poland, Rumania, Latvia, Estonia, and Lithuania. We shall therefore expand our horizons when dealing with the *Shoah*, and include elements of the Jewish experience in Poland and in the Baltic States.

For a general emotional orientation to this period *Night* by Elie Weisel is highly recommended. The special Soviet dimension to the *Shoah* is well covered in *The Holocaust* by Nora Levin (Thomas Y. Crowell Company, New York, 1968).

EINSATZGRUPPEN

The *Shoah* came to the Jews of the USSR in a particularly brutal and devastating fashion. With the German invasion of the Soviet Union in June, 1941, millions of Soviet Jewish citizens found themselves trapped in what had once been the old Tsarist Pale of Settlement. Many were evacuated by the Soviet government to Central Asia. Those who were caught by the advancing German army were doomed.

The means for the destruction of the Jews in the occupied regions were special roving military and SS units called *Einsatzgruppen* ("special groups"). Each of the four units, lettered A, B, C, and D, operated in a different region of the continually expanding Russian front. The full strength of one of these units was about 3,000 men, including Lithuanians, Estonians, Ukrainians, and Rumanians as auxiliaries. These units murdered over 1,200,000 Jews in places such as Babi Yar near Kiev, and Ponary on the outskirts of Vilna.

The following documents are the German orders drafted to define the role of these *Einsatzgruppen*.

> From: Field Marshal Keitel, Chief of OKW (Army General Staff)
> Date: 13 March 1941
> Re: Instructions on Special Matters attached to Directive No. 21 (Barbarossa—invasion of USSR)

Paragraph 2(b)

In order to prepare the political and administrative organization the Reichsfurer-SS has been given by the Fuhrer certain special tasks within the operations zone of the army; these stem from the necessity finally to settle the conflict between the two opposing political systems. Within the framework of these tasks the Reichsfurer-SS will act independently and on his own responsibility. This is, however, without prejudice to the over-riding plenary power hereby accorded the Commander-in-Chief, Army. . . .

From: Reinhardt Heydrich, Chief RSHA (*Gestapo* and police)
Date: 2 July 1941
Re: Summary of Basic Instructions to *Einsatzgruppen*

Paragraph 4 Executions

The following will be executed:
all officials of the Comitern (most of these will certainly be career politicians);
officials of senior and middle rank and "extremists" in the party, the central committee, and the provisional and district committees;
the Peoples' Commissars;
Jews in the service of the Party or the State;
other extremist elements (saboteurs, propagandists, snipers, assassins, agitators, etc.);
No steps will be taken to interfere with any purges that may be initiated by the anti-Communist or anti-Jewish elements in the newly occupied territories. On the contrary, they are to be secretly encouraged. At the same time every precaution must be taken to ensure that those who engage in "self-defense" actions are not subsequently able to plead that they were acting under orders or had been promised political protection. . . .

For further background, cf. Baron, pp. 295-301.

Helmut Krausnick in his article "The Persecution of the Jews" in *The Anatomy of the SS State* adds:

> There can be no doubt, in spite of the emphasis on the execution of Jews in the service of the Party or the State in this written memorandum, that the *Einsatzgruppen* had verbal orders to shoot all Jews. According to the testimony of a commander, already by June, 1941 Heydrich himself had explained to the commander of the *Einsatzgruppen* that "Judaism in the east is the source of Bolshevism and must therefore be wiped out in accordance with the *Fuehrer's* aims."

Questions to Consider

1. How did the *Shoah* in the Soviet Union differ from that of other lands? How did the *Einsatzgruppen* operate in their job of killing Jews?

2. What range of powers did Keitel's orders grant to the special units? How did they go about their functions?

3. At what other periods in history did the ruling powers declare an "open season" on Jews as Heydrich did in July, 1941? Were Hitler's plans for the Jews of Russia unique in Russian-Jewish history?

RUSSIA AT WAR

Alexander Werth was born in St. Petersburg in 1901, and emigrated to England after the Russian revolutions. In 1941 he returned to the Soviet Union as a correspondent for the *Sunday Times* and BBC commentator, and stayed until 1948. His *Russia at War 1941-1945* is the classic work on World War II from the vantage point of Moscow. Werth's unique background makes his descriptions of various Jewish scenes in wartime Russia especially valuable.

Each of the following three selections focuses on a different facet of the *Shoah*.

"RUSSO-UKRAINIAN UNITY"

At the end of 1943, while recapturing the Ukraine from the Nazis, the Red Army instituted a new high decoration, the Order of Bogdan Chmelnitsky. The army newspaper *Red Star* described the award thusly:

"A Knight of the Order of Bogdan Chmelnitsky—that is a proud title. The life of Bogdan Chmelnitsky is an example of the decisive struggle for the brotherly union of the Ukrainian people and its elder brother, the Russian people. Chmelnitsky clearly realized that the free and prosperous development of the Ukraine was possible only in the closest union with Russia. The Soviet people who finally completed the union of all Ukrainian lands into one mighty state, under the Red Banner of the Soviets, particularly value Bogdan Chmelnitsky's immortal deed."

The Chmelnitsky order caused some embarrassment when a number of Russian officers of Jewish race refused the Chmelnitsky order on the grounds the glorious Hetman had been guilty of a considerable number of pogroms.

Questions to Consider

1. What was the extent of the participation of Jews in the Red Army during World War II? What is the Jewish presence today in the ranks of the Red Army officer corps?
2. What is your reaction to their refusal? Was it justified?
3. Are there any awards which you would refuse because of their associations?

"THE LIBERATION OF MAIDANEK: A POLISH REACTION"

At the end of August, 1944, Werth visited Lublin, Poland, a city in the shadow of the death camp Maidanek, only two miles away. The Red Army liberated a number of concentration and extermination camps in Poland on their march westward. "When the wind blew from the east it brought with it the stench of burning human flesh from the crematoria chimneys." He spoke to a certain Polish professor who had been one of the few intellectuals not killed by the Nazis.

Werth tells that the professor began to talk about Maidanek, where over one and a half million people had been murdered—many Poles among them, but, above all, Jews.

> "What," I asked, "has been the attitude of the Polish people to the massacre of millions of Jews?"

"This is a very tricky subject; let's face it," said the professor. "Owing to a number of historical processes, such as the Tsarist government's Jewish policy of confining most of the Jews in the Russian Empire to Poland, we have had far too many Jews here. Our retail trade was entirely in Jewish hands. They also played an unduly large part in other walks of life. There is no doubt that the Polish people wanted the number of Jews in Poland reduced. They wanted part of them to emigrate to America, to Palestine, or perhaps to Madagascar; there was a scheme before the war. But that was one thing," he added a little glibly, "What the Germans did is quite another thing, and this, I can tell you, genuinely revolted every one of our people...."

Questions to Consider

1. How do you react to the logic of the professor? How does he justify the Polish opinions of the Jews?
2. Was the atmosphere in Poland in the years 1934-1939, 1939-1945, and 1945-present, pro- or anti-Semitic?
3. Are there people in America today who feel similarly about the Jews? In your opinion, is the status of Jews in America basically a settled and stable one, or is our position more tenuous? Discuss.
4. What was the position of the government of the United States in the pre-War period regarding open immigration? How did this policy affect the scope and magnitude of the *Shoah?*

"THE LIBERATION OF MAIDANEK: THE RUSSIAN REACTION"

Maidanek holds a very special place in the Soviet-German war.

As they advanced, the Russians had been learning more and more of German atrocities and the enormous number of killings. But, somehow, all this killing was spread over relatively wide areas, and though it added up to far, far more than Maidanek, it did not have the vast monumental, "industrial" quality of that unbelievable Death Factory two miles from Lublin.

"Unbelievable" it was: when I sent the BBC a detailed report on Maidanek in August, 1944, they refused to use it; they thought it was a Russian propaganda stunt, and it was not till the discovery in the west of Buchenwald, Dachau, and Belson that they were convinced that Maidanek and Auschwitz were also genuine. . . .

The Russians discovered Maidanek on July 23, the very day they entered Lublin. About a week later Simonov described it all in *Pravda;* but most of the Western press ignored his account. But in Russia the effect was devastating. Everybody had heard of Babi Yar and thousands of other German atrocities; but this was something even more staggering. It brought into sharper focus than anything else had done, the real nature, scope and consequences of the Nazi regime in action. For here was a vast industrial undertaking in which thousands of "ordinary" Germans had made it a full-time job to murder millions of other people in a sort of mass orgy of professional sadism, or worse still, with the business-like conviction that *this was a job like any other.* The effect of Maidanek was to be enormous, not least in the Red Army. Thousands of Russian soldiers were made to visit it.

Questions to Consider

1. How many death camps were there in Poland? What were their names and where were they located?
2. What does the BBC reaction indicate about the understanding of the *Shoah* by the people of that time?
3. How did the world first find out about the *Shoah?*
4. If you had been the news editor of the BBC in London in August, 1944, would you have allowed the broadcast of Werth's story? Why did the BBC not?
5. What connotations does the term "fascism" have today in the contemporary Soviet Union? In the United States?

THE JEWISH ANTI-FASCIST COMMITTEE

In an effort to gain Jewish support, both within the Soviet Union and throughout the world, Stalin organized the Jewish Anti-Fascist Committee in April, 1942. Its members included some of the leading Yiddish writers and novelists of the Soviet Union.

The first and virtually only official contact with the Jews of the Soviet Union and American Jewry came as a result of this Committee's work. After some twenty-six years of no ties with world Jewry being allowed, in May, 1943 an official Soviet delegation arrived in the United States. Its members included the actor Shlomo Michoels of the Jewish State Theater in Moscow, and the poet Itzik Feffer. They were enthusiastically and warmly greeted by the American Jewish and general communities. Feffer subsequently reported that they toured 46 cities in the United States, Canada, and Mexico, and spoke to audiences of some half-a-million Jews.

During this same period, the Soviet authorities allowed many Jews to flee as refugees into the heartland of Russia, Central Asia, and there to constitute some forms of Jewish life. This policy of resettlement permitted many Polish and Russian Jews to survive the Nazi Holocaust.

The following is an appeal of May, 1942, made at the second conference of the Committee, and broadcast to the West from Moscow. It is addressed to "The Jews of the United States, England, Canada, Mexico, Palestine, Argentine, Brazil, Uruguay, South Africa, Australia, etc."

Jews in all parts of the world! Remember that through your oath and your participation in the drive for tanks and aeroplanes for the heroic Red Army you ensure your own existence and the existence of your families, and you help to save the Jewish people from extermination.

We, your Soviet Brethren, appeal to you, Jews of the whole world! Together let us bring to the ranks of the people the call of the great fighters of the Jewish people and the great Jewish scientists—the names of Yehuda Halevi, Bar-Kochba, Baruch Spinoza, Heinrich Heine, Shalom Aleichem, J. I. Peretz, Mendele Mocher Sforim and others. Let us give them the names of the Jewish heroes in the patriotic war—Major General Jacob Kreizer and others. Together with the demands for the general mobilization of the Jews in the world we call on every Jew to take an oath on the anniversary of Germany's attack on Russia on the 22nd of June, to avenge my brothers and sisters who were tortured, burnt and buried alive in all the villages and towns which were destroyed and ruined.

Questions to Consider

1. Why was this appeal made? Would not the Jews have supported the Red Army in any event? What might this indicate about Stalin's image of the place of the Jewish people in the world?

2. If you were asked to list "great fighters of the Jewish people and great Jewish scientists" which names would you have included? Why were the particular names chosen in this appeal?

3. What specific kind of support is the Jewish Anti-Fascist Committee requesting from world Jewry?

For further background, cf. Baron, pp. 304-307.

4. Does this appeal represent a continuation or a change in Soviet policy regarding the Jews? How did Stalin treat nationality problems during the "Great Patriotic War" (World War II)?

5. What was the final fate of the Committee and of its major leaders in particular?

6. In recent years, the State of Israel has appealed to Jews of the United States for many forms of support. How has American Jewry responded? What should our response be?

JEWISH RESISTANCE: THE PARTISANS

After the initial shock of the German invasion had passed, a series of partisan groups began to form in the occupied territories. Misha Gildenman, a Jewish engineer from the Soviet Ukraine, became famous as a Soviet Jewish partisan commander. Around the region of Zhitomer in the Ukraine he was known as "Dyadya Misha" (Uncle Misha), where he directed his forces for more than two years. In many other areas in the front, notably around Bialystok, Vilna, and the forests of White Russia, Jewish partisan units functioned.

The following is a description of the plans for a pre-*Purim* raid by a group of these Jewish partisans. The unit has been assigned to blow up a German train carrying fliers to the battle area.

> "That is all. Be careful, be brave, do not think of death and be confident of victory. The sky is overcast. That means it will be a very dark night. Get ready, because in an hour from now you will be on your way."
>
> The partisans peered earnestly into the fire. Night fell quickly. One of the partisans tossed some fresh pine branches on the fire. They crackled and burned brightly, illuminating the old pine trees standing nearby, their bent branches laden with snow.
>
> David rolled a thick cigarette for himself in a piece of German newspaper and lighted it up with a burning twig he pulled from the fire. Then he inhaled the strong tobacco deeply several times and the serious expression on his face changed to a genial smile. He spat vigorously and turned

to his comrades: "Why are you sitting here on your haunches? Don't you know that today is the Eve of *Purim?* Who would have thought that David of Yarevitch, the transport worker, or David, the coachman, as he was once called, would, on the Eve of *Purim*, be hiding out in the woods, armed with grenades, like a forest robber, and prepare to blow up a train carrying German fliers?"

Suddenly he became serious again and, staring thoughtfully ahead of him, spoke, as though to himself: "I can see my serge *kaftan*. . . . We have returned from the synagogue and brought home with us a guest. . . . The room is brightly lit, warm and spic-and-span. . . . The table is covered with a snow-white tablecloth . . . the candles are burning in the polished shining brass candlesticks. . . . On the table lies a big *Purim* twist . . . a platter of tasty carp and a deep bowl of compote. . . .

"My wife, Sarah," David continued, "wearing a white apron and a red handkerchief over her black curly hair, invites us to the table. . . . On my knees I hold my two dear children." David fell silent a moment and sighed deeply. "The Germans have murdered them all!" He tossed his cigarette butt into the fire and, raising his clenched fists, cried out, "Revenge! Jews, we must avenge every drop of Jewish blood spilled at the hands of the Germans!"

A hush fell over the partisans. Only the crackling of the dry branches in the fire and the howling of the wolves in the distance could be heard from time to time.

"Better let us talk of our task ahead," David said. "We are going to blow up an armored train. I can just see them, the well-fed, clean-shaven Germans, sitting in their warm compartments, the farewell speeches of their teachers still ringing in their ears. They are on their way to Kursk to take over the planes . . . they are daring, courageous. . . . They think they will enter their steel birds, with the black and white swastikas on the wings, fly over Moscow and drop their bombs. Already they see the Iron Cross and other decorations pinned on their uniforms. . . . But I, the coachman of Yarevitch, think differently. . . . And I will lay the mine under the little bridge. . . . And my report to Dyadya Misha will be as follows: 'The assignment you have given me has been carried out. The armored train—its 22 cars and locomotives were blown up and the 333 German fliers have, in honor of *Purim*, suffered Haman's fate. . . .' "

The partisans were so spellbound by David's imaginary description of the sabotage act they were about to carry out that they remained silent for some time. Then David gave the command: "Fellows, time to go!"

The partisans rose eagerly from their places and began to tighten their belts, check their weapons, and put the rags into their knapsacks.

"And now let us say a prayer for the journey," David said, turning to his comrades. He took out a small prayer book from his leather holster and in a pleasant voice began to say: "May Thy Will Be Done. . . ." Many of the partisans repeated the prayer after him silently. It was a strange scene—a groups of Jews, armed with rifles and hand grenades, praying in the secrecy of a forest.

With great fervor David repeated twice the words of the prayer.

"Shield us from every foe." He then pointed to the box containing the mine, which lay near him, and said to Motele of Berznitz, "Tie the *shalachmonuth* (Purim gift) around my back, do so that it will not rub against my shoulders. . . . All is ready. We can go."

Questions to Consider

1. How did the Jewish partisan movement originate? What was its chain of command? Who were some of its most famous commanders?

2. Why did the partisans feel so strongly about the Germans? What major motivation seems to have dictated their actions?

3. What is your reaction to David's call for "Revenge!"? Do you feel that strongly about anyone or anything in the contemporary world? Is vengeance a feeling to be encouraged or repressed?

4. How widespread was this form of Jewish resistance? What prevented more Jews from joining the partisan movement?

THE BLACKBOOK

The *Shoah* for European Jewry ended with the capture of Berlin by the Soviet forces and the surrender of the German Army to the Allies in May, 1945. The Jews of the USSR began to return to their homes from the interior of Russia and Central Asia, from their hiding places in the forests, from the liberated ghettos and death camps, and from the ranks of the Red Army and Partisan units. Many did not return. Jewish life, particularly in Eastern Europe, had been devastated. Great Jewish population centers in Rumania, Hungary, Czechoslovakia, Poland, and the western regions of the Soviet Union, were no more.

The following numbers can only serve as a pale reminder to the extent of devastation which befell the Jews of Europe in the years 1933-1945. Note that after Poland, the Jewish community of the USSR suffered the greatest losses.

The figures are taken from the *American Jewish Yearbook* and *The Blackbook of Localities Whose Jewish Population Was Exterminated By the Nazis* (published by "The Martyr's and Heroes Remembrance Authority of the State of Israel —*Yad Vashem*").

EXTERMINATION OF THE JEWISH POPULATION OF EUROPE

Country	Number of Jews Killed
Germany (1937 frontiers)	200,000
Austria	40,000
Czechoslovakia (1937 frontiers)	300,000

THE SHOAH

Country	Number of Jews Killed
Denmark	1,500
France	130,000
Belgium	40,000
Luxembourg	3,000
Norway	1,000
Netherlands	120,000
Italy	20,000
Yugoslavia	65,000
Greece	60,000
Bulgaria (pre-1941 frontiers)	5,000
Rumania (pre-1940 frontiers)	420,000
Hungary (1938 frontiers)	200,000
Poland (1939 frontiers)	2,900,000
USSR (pre-1939 frontiers)	1,000,000
Soviet Latvia	85,000
Soviet Lithuania	135,000
	5,925,500

NUMBER OF LOCALITIES MADE *"JUDENREIN"* (DEVOID OF JEWS) BY THE NAZIS

Austria	769
Czechoslovakia	4,000
Estonia	50
Germany	3,383
Greece	48
Hungary	2,462
Latvia	413
Lithuania	295
Luxembourg	12
Netherlands	395
Norway	28
Poland	16,782
Rumania	3,013
USSR	1,086
Yugoslavia	678
	33,914

Questions to Consider

1. What percentage of the Jews of each of the countries of Europe had been annihilated during the *Shoah?* How has the *Shoah* affected the nature and quality of Jewish life in these countries today, some 30 years after the War?

2. If you were teaching a class, and were faced with these statistics, how would you make them more immediate and more meaningful for your students?

3. In what ways can we make the message and memory of the *Shoah* more meaningful to us, and more a part of our lives?

4. As Jews, what should we do differently in our lives so that the murder of European Jewry should not have been in vain?

THE *MITZVAH* OF REMEMBERING

Although there have been many destructions and catastrophes in Jewish history, none has reached the magnitude of the *Shoah* which befell European Jewry during the years 1933-1945. The annihilation of nearly 34,000 communities, the murder of 6,000,000 Jews and the ravaging of European Jewish life is, for most of us, an inconceivable reality. For the overwhelming number of European cities, all that remained of their once flourishing and thriving Jewish populations were memories.

The Jewish people is heir to many memories. Some reflect the glories and highpoints of Jewish history, others, the moments of tragedy. The three Pilgrimage Holidays each focus on one particular memory out of the Jewish past—the Exodus from Egypt (*Pesach*), the receiving of the Torah on Mount Sinai (*Shavuot*), and living in the wilderness (*Sukkot*). The Ninth of Av and others of the fast days, recall the periods of destruction and sadness.

In his classic work, *The Book of the Commandments* (*Sefer Hamitzvot*), Maimonides singles out one particular act of wanton destruction as worthy of remembering. Echoing the Biblical mandate, he feels that the nature of the attack which Amalek launched on the Jewish people was so savage and despicable, as to evoke the deepest and most elementary of human emotions.

Consider the following from Maimonides:

REMEMBERING THE EVIL DEEDS OF AMALEK

By which we are commanded to remember that which Amalek did to us, by attacking us without provocation. We are to speak of this constantly, and to arouse and incite others to make war upon them, and to encourage men to hate them, in order that the event not be forgotten, and that the hatred of them not be weakened nor lessened with the passing of time.

This command is contained in the words of the Torah: "Remember that which Amalek did to you" (Deuteronomy 25:17). The *Sifre* comments: "Remember that which Amalek did to you"—in the spoken word; "do not forget"—in your heart. In other words, say those kinds of things that will ensure that men will not remove this hate from their hearts.

Questions to Consider

1. What was Amalek and what did it do?
2. What is the place of "hatred" in the Jewish tradition? What kind of hatreds are rejected? How would you balance the contemporary American emphasis on "love" with this command?
3. How would you apply this command to Nazi Germany? Do you believe that Jews should boycott modern-day Germany and German-produced goods? Why or why not?
4. Could another *Shoah* happen again? What should be our role in insuring that it does not?

SOVIET JEWRY UNIT

The Black Years and Contemporary Soviet Jewry

INTRODUCTION

The contemporary position of the Soviet government regarding the Soviet Jews was indelibly stamped during the final years of Stalin, the so-called "Black Years." In this final historical unit we will discuss the immediate events leading up to the contemporary status of Soviet Jews. We will be with Golda Meir in Moscow in 1948, and live through the terror of the "Doctor's Plot." We will examine the current condition of Soviet Jewish culture, construct our own model Jewish community, make plans for a visit to the Soviet Union, join Russian Jews immigrating to Israel, and feel the response of the Soviet government.

In preparation for this unit, review *The Jews of Silence* by Elie Wiesel, and other diaries and descriptions of the contemporary Soviet Jewish scene. *Between Hammer and Sickle* by Arie Eliav is especially recommended. Focus particularly on the experiences of tourists to the Soviet Union.

THE BLACK YEARS: GOLDA MEIR IN MOSCOW

For the Jews of the Soviet Union, 1948 marked a major and tragic turning point. Members of the Jewish Anti-Fascist Committee were rounded up, and a period of repression unknown even since Tsarist days began. The major Yiddish publishing house was closed. Jewish libraries, the last Yiddish schools, professional theaters, and all vestiges of Soviet Jewish culture were liquidated. Hundreds of Soviet Jewish writers, poets, actors, painters, sculptors, and musicians were exiled to Siberia or deprived of their livelihoods. Most of the prisoners died in labor camps. In the 1948-1953 period, over 350 Jewish officers of high rank in the Red Army were retired, and only one Jew remained a member of the ruling Soviet Politbureau.

With the executions that followed, the total impact of these years was such that they became infamously known as the "Black Years" of Soviet Jewry.

Most commentators suggest that the visit of Golda Meir (then Golda Meyerson) to Moscow as the first ambassador of the newborn State of Israel was the crucial catalytic event of that decisive period.

The following is a description of the High Holiday season in Moscow in 5708, 1948.

> Jewish enthusiasm reached its peak with the arrival of the Israel Legation to Moscow, headed by Mrs. Golda Meyerson. The flag of the State of Israel above the legation

building was a gripping symbol for many Jews. Jewish patriotism now had a tangible, national, Israel significance. No practical expression, to be sure, was given to it as yet. Jewish emigration was not yet being permitted, but deep in their hearts grew the hope that henceforward the obstacles would be removed from the paths of those who wished to join their kinsfolk, and that immigration to the State of Israel would now be permitted. Hopes also grew of the liberation of Zionist prisoners who had suffered bitter exile for many years.

Tens of thousands of Jews, religious and non-religious alike, made their way to the Great Synagogue in Moscow where the Legation staff came to pray on Sabbaths and Festivals. The Central Synagogue was too small to contain all the Jews who came to welcome the Minister there on the New Year and Day of Atonement of 5708 (1948). Masses of Jews who did not succeed in entering the synagogue crowded round it, waiting for the departure of the Minister and her suite. When they appeared on the threshhold of the synagogue on New Year's Day at the close of the prayers, they were welcomed with enthusiastic cheers. From the midst of the crowd came the cry in Hebrew "The Jewish People continues to live!" Mrs. Golda Meyerson stopped for a few moments while the excited crowd virtually blocked her way, waiting for her to speak. "I thank you for having remained Jews," she said in Yiddish. A tremor of consolation and joy passed through those assembled, the circle opened of itself, and the Minister and her suite were permitted to go on their way.

For many years Moscow had not seen such a demonstration as when the Jewish residents of the city came to greet the emissaries of the State of Israel. It was an unforgettable experience for Soviet Jewry. On "Kol Nidrei" night, the Eve of Atonement, a large crowd gathered afresh within

---

For further background, cf. Baron, pp. 309-326.

and around the synagogue. When the Legation staff came out after the prayers, a kind of procession organized itself and accompanied them to their temporary lodging in the Metropol Hotel. Once more the cry "The Jewish People continues to live!" was heard. All the way the procession was accompanied by a group of police who kept order. At the sight of the strange procession many passers-by stopped in the streets, astonishment written on their faces.

Questions to Consider

1. Why did the Jews of the Soviet Union greet Mrs. Meir so enthusiastically? What has been the recent reception of Israeli diplomats in the United States?

2. What did this reception by the Jews of Moscow indicate and signify to the Russian authorities?

3. What was the mood in the Kremlin in 1948 regarding the West and all things Western?

4. How did the Soviet treatment of the Soviet Jews fit into this unfolding cold war pattern?

THE BLACK YEARS: THE "DOCTOR'S PLOT"

This tragic and bloody period neared completion with the August 12, 1952 execution of 24 of the remaining prominent Jewish writers and poets, including Peretz Markish, Itzik Feffer and David Bergelson. All were charged with being "enemies of the USSR, agents of American imperialism and burgeois nationalist Zionism. . . ."

One final tragic act remained to be played. In 1953, the last year of Stalin's life, a group of Jewish physicians was arrested and accused of a so-called "Doctor's Plot" to assassinate members of the Soviet hierarchy. The doctors were arrested, imprisoned, and many were tortured.

The following editorials and articles, from the front pages of the official Communist Party newspaper *Pravda,* present the venom and accusations of this campaign.

> Whom did these monsters (the Jewish doctors) serve? Who directed the criminal terrorist and wretching activity of these vile traitors to the motherland? . . . It has been established that all the participants in the terrorist group of doctors were enrolled in foreign intelligence services, sold them their bodies and souls, were their hired, paid agents. . . . The dirty face of this Zionist espionage organization (Joint), concealing its foul work under a mask of charity, has been completely exposed. . . . Exposure of the band of poisoner-doctors is a blow at the international Jewish Zionist organization. Now all can see what charitable friends of peace hide under the "Joint" letterhead. . . .

The Soviet people wrathfully and indignantly condemn the criminal band of murderers and their foreign masters. They will crush like loathsome vermin the despised hirelings who sold themselves for dollars and pounds sterling. As for the inspirers of these hired murderers, they may rest assured that vengeance will not pass them by but will find a path to them. . . .

The crimes of the terrorist group of saboteur-doctors . . . show that there is no crime to which the imperialists will not descend. . . . Most of the participants in this group were enlisted by a branch of the American intelligence service—the international Jewish bourgeois nationalist organization "Joint."

Zionism has become the tool of the American-British warmongers. . . . The subversives in white gowns attempted to undermine the health of leading Soviet military cadres, to put them out of action, and to weaken the country's defense.

Questions to Consider

1. How do you react upon reading such charges? How would you feel if those close to you were accused in the editorial of a leading American newspaper of similar charges?

2. How did this episode affect the ethos (basic spiritual character) of Soviet Jewry? What would be the effect in America if Jewish doctors were arrested for planning the assassination of the President and the Administration? What effect would this have on American Jewry?

3. Some people credit the internal Soviet Jewish activism since 1967, as the by-product of the Six Day War. What other factors could help to explain these phenomena? Would someone who had personally experienced Stalin's "Black

Years" be more or less inclined to protest the Soviet government, even 20 years later?

4. What is the "Joint?" Of what is it accused? Is your national loyalty questioned because of the organizations with which you identify or support?

5. What motivated Stalin to initiate the "Black Years?" What had he to gain from a "Doctors Plot?"

POST-WAR SOVIET YIDDISH PUBLISHING

The effects of the "Black Years" lingered on far after Stalin's death in March, 1953. Jewish participation in the leadership levels of the ruling Communist Party, the Soviet state bureaucracy, and the Soviet Army was virtually eliminated. Psychologically, the effects were far greater than those of the McCarthy era in the American social experience, which occurred at the same time as the peak of Stalin's Black Years. The basic character of Soviet Jewry had been drastically marked and altered.

The effects were most devastating in the cultural sphere. All that had been destroyed during the 1948-1953 period was not restored. Yiddish became a virtual non-language, even though fully 20% of the Soviet Jewish population declared it to be their "mother tongue." After the lapse of a dozen years, one Yiddish language publication began to appear in 1961 *Sovetish Heymland* ("Soviet Homeland"). Edited by Aaron Vergelis, the journal reflects a standard Soviet ideology.

The following are the publishing statistics for Yiddish publications in the USSR from the *Shoah* through the mid-1960's.

Year	Number of Yiddish Books and Pamphlets	Yiddish Newspapers and Periodicals
1942	2	1
1943	24	1
1944	18	1
1945	14	2
1946	19	3
1947	52	5

Year	Number of Yiddish Books and Pamphlets	Yiddish Newspapers and Periodicals
1948	60	5
1949	0	0
1950	0	0
1951	0	0
1952	0	0
1953	0	0
1954	0	0
1955	0	0
1956	0	0
1957	0	0
1958	0	0
1959	3	0
1960	1	0
1961	2	1 (bimonthly)
1962	1	1
1963	0	1
1964	1	1
1965	5	1 (monthly)

Questions to Consider

1. How do these figures compare with the publication statistics of the 1917-1941 period?

2. What factors, in addition to official Soviet government disfavor, have contributed to the decline of Yiddish publishing since 1948?

3. What do these Yiddish publication statistics indicate about the Jewish nationality policy of the Soviet Union since the *Shoah?*

4. What is the extent and scope of Jewish publications in the United States today? Which topics seem to be of greatest interest? Which American Jewish newspapers and periodicals are most widely read?

THE USE OF YIDDISH IN THE SOVIET UNION

There is no doubt that the number of Yiddish speakers in the Soviet Union is on the decline. In addition to the demographic aspect of this problem, the fact that Yiddish speakers are aging and dying, other factors contribute to this situation. Even in America today the number of Yiddish speakers is not on the rise. What is the difference between the reasons for the decline of Yiddish speakers in the Soviet Union and in the United States? How would you account for this decline in both countries?

The following are the number of Soviet Jews who declared Yiddish to be their "Mother Tongue" in the 1959 Soviet census (in thousands).

Name of Republic	# of Ashkenazim	# Declaring Yiddish	% Declaring
Russian (RSFSR)	858	102	11.9
Ukrainian	848	142	16.9
Belorussian	150	33	22.0
Moldavian	95	48	50.0
Uzbek	66	28	42.4
Georgian	15	2	13.3
Azerbaijan	30	6	20.0
Latvian	37	18	48.6
Kazakstan	28	6	21.4
Lithuanian	25	17	68.0
Tadzhikistan	11	2	18.2
Estonian	5	1	20.0
Turkmenistan	4	1	25.0
Armenian	1	0	00.0
Kirghiz	0	0	00.0

Questions to Consider

1. Why do Lithuania, Moldavia, and Latvia have the highest percentage of declared Yiddish speakers? What do they have in common?

2. Why do the Russian and Ukrainian Republics have the lowest (large-sized) percentage of Yiddish speakers? What do they share in common?

3. How did Yiddish speaking Jews find their way to such places as Uzbekistan, Georgia, Azerbaijan, Kazakstan, Tadzhikistan, and Turkmenistan?

4. How does the Soviet government treat Jews differently depending on from what regions of the country they come? How is this expressed, especially in the government's religious and emigration policies?

6. What is to be the future and fate of Yiddish in the Soviet Union? What is to be the future and fate of Yiddish in the United States?

7. Many scholars feel that the official Soviet Jewish population census figures are inaccurate, often significantly lower than their true numbers. How would you support or refute this view?

SOVIET JEWRY IN THE 1960'S: "BABI YAR"

In the immediate post-war period, many hoped that a full, vibrant, albeit non-religious, Jewish life in the USSR would be revived. The Black Years and Khrushchev period which followed severely dampened those expectations. However, the possibility did still exist for a limited, though viable, Russian Jewish community, presumably modeled on the Jewish life of the 1920's and 1930's (Yiddish speaking, non-religious, and non-Zionist).

In the 1960's, token gestures were made by the Soviet authorities in this direction, including the publication in 1961 of a Yiddish periodical *Sovetish Heymland*, Yiddish language concerts, some translations of Yiddish writers into Russian, and the issuing of a commemorative stamp on the centennial of Shalom Aleichem's birth. However, these were more than balanced by the decline in the number of synagogues in the USSR between 1956 and 1965 from 450 to 96, the appearance of a blatantly anti-Semitic book in 1963 (*Judaism Without Embellishment* by T. K. Kichko, published by the Ukrainian Academy of Sciences), and the continued suppression of Yiddish schools and publications.

The publication of Yevgeni Yevtushenko's poem "Babi Yar" in the *Literaturnaya Gazeta* on September 19, 1961 signalled to the world that the Soviet government's policy towards the Jews had not changed for the better. The freeze on Jewish life was to be continued.

For further background, cf. Baron, pp. 331-344.

At issue was the erection of a memorial marker at a site of Jewish martyrdom during the *Shoah*. The poem focused on a mile-long, 50 foot wide ditch, on the outskirts of Kiev, where, on September 29-30, 1941, the Nazis murdered over 33,000 Jewish men, women and children. By the end of the German occupation of Kiev, over 100,000 people had been murdered there, most of them Jews. For many years no monument or even marker commemorated the Jewish martyrs. A more recently added stone marks the death of "Soviet citizens," ignoring all mention of their being Jews.

BABI YAR

No gravestone stands on Babi Yar.
Only coarse earth heaped roughly on the gash.
Such dread comes over me; I feel so old,
Old as the Jews. Today I am a Jew . . .
Now I go wandering an Egyptian slave;
And now I perish, splayed upon the cross.

The marks of nails are still upon my flesh.
And I am Dreyfus whom the gentry hound:
I am behind the bars, caught in a ring;
Belied, denounced and spat upon I stand,
While dainty ladies in their lacy frills
Squealing, poke parasols into my face.

I am that little boy in Bialystok
Whose blood flows, spreading darkly on the floor.
The rowdy lords of the saloon make sport,
Reeking alike of vodka and of leek.
Booted aside, weak, helpless, I, the child
Who begs in vain while the pogromchik mob
Guffaws and shouts "Save Russia, beat the Jews!"
The shopman's blow fall on my mother's back.

O my own people, my own Russian folk,
Believers in the brotherhood of man!
But dirty hands too often dare to raise
The banner of your pure and lofty name.
I know the goodness of my native land.
How vile that anti-Semites shamelessly
Preen themselves in the words that they debase:
"The Union of the Russian People."

Now in this moment, I am Anna Frank,
Frail and transparent as an April twig.
I love as she; I need no ready phrases ...
Only to look into each other's eyes!
How little can we sense, how little see ...
Leaves are forbidden us, the sky forbidden ...
Yet how much still remains; how strangely sweet
To hold each other close in the dark room.
They come? No, do not fear. These are the gates
Of spring; she bursts into this gloom.
Come to me; quickly; let me kiss your lips ...
They break the door? No, no, the ice is breaking.

On Babi Yar weeds rustle; the tall trees
Like judges loom and threaten ...
All screams in silence; I take off my cap
And feel that I am slowly turning gray.
And I too have become a soundless cry
Over the thousands that lie buried here.
I am each old man slaughtered, each child shot.
None of me will forget.

Let the glad "internationale" blare forth
When earth's last anti-Semite lies in earth.
No drop of Jewish blood flows in my veins,
But anti-Semites with a dull, gnarled hate
Detest me like a Jew.
O know me truly Russian through their hate!

Questions to Consider

1. Which scenes of Jewish history does Yevtushenko evoke in the poem? How does he convey the impact of the pogrom?

2. To what about Babi Yar does he object? Why?

3. What is the official Soviet position concerning anti-Semitism and anti-Semitic behavior?

4. What is the status of other memorials to Jewish martyrs or of Jewish life in the Soviet Union?

5. Why did the publication of Babi Yar create such a sensation, and why is the poem so popular?

SOVIET JEWRY IN THE 1970'S: JEWISH ACTIVISTS CHALLENGE THE SOVIET GOVERNMENT

Beginning in 1968, Soviet Jews, first as isolated individuals, and then as organized groups, began to militate to leave the Soviet Union. Most prominent in these activities were younger Jews, who resided in the Baltic States, and the newly Sovietized cities of the western border of the Russian Republic and the Ukraine. Although few in numbers, their voices began to be heard in the West and in Israel. Certainly the Six-Day War of June, 1967 acted as a major catalyst for this ferment.

Many legal avenues of protest under Soviet law were utilized. Petitions were written, letters were sent, visas were applied for. Increasingly restive, some attempted more activist methods, including sit-ins and demonstrations (at sites of Jewish martyrdom including Babi Yar in Kiev, and Ponary near Vilna). Clandestine *Ulpanim* were organized, and Jewish and Israeli national holidays were openly celebrated.

The Soviet government responded on a number of fronts. After often being harassed and intimidated, numbers of Soviet Jews were allowed to exit to Israel. An "education tax" was levied to discourage trained technicians and professionals from leaving. Police raids were conducted at the home of particularly active Zionists. Some Soviet Jews appeared at government sponsored press conferences to denounce those who wished to leave, and affirmed their loyalty to the Soviet

State. In general, the Soviet government seemed to be pursuing a policy of limiting the influence of the most outspoken and unassimilatable elements in the USSR.

Some Jews became desperate. In the summer of 1970, the Soviet press and authorities reported the arrest of a group of Soviet citizens for the attempted hijacking of a Soviet airplane to leave the USSR and reach Israel. The 11 defendants (2 of them non-Jews) were indicted for high treason, conspiracy, grand larceny, and anti-Soviet agitation and propaganda. In fact, all were apprehended by the KGB (Soviet secret police) before they boarded the airplane in question. The following selection is taken from an unofficial transcript of the December 15-24, 1970 Leningrad trial.

The Leningrad prosecuting attorney (referred to as the Procurator) Solovyev demanded the death penalty for Mark Dymshits and Edward Kuznetsov. Silva Zalmonson, one of the accused conspirators and the only woman, responded in her final statement to the court:

> I can't get over it. . . . I am stunned by the penalties the procurator has demanded. The procurator has now proposed that heads should roll for *something that has not been done*. And if the court agrees then such wonderful people as Dymshits and Kuznetsov will die. I don't think that Soviet law can consider one's "intention" to live in another country "treason" and I am convinced that the law ought to bring to court those who *unlawfully deny our right* to live where we want to.
>
> Let the court at least take into consideration that *if we were allowed to leave* there would be no "criminal collusion" which has caused so much suffering to us and even greater distress to our families.
>
> Israel is the country with which we Jews are bound spiritually and historically. I hope that the government of the

USSR will soon provide a favorable solution to this problem. We shall never abandon the dream of being united with our people in our ancient homeland. Some of us did not believe in the success of the escape or believed in it very slightly. Already at the Finland Station (in Leningrad) we noticed that we were being followed, but we could no longer go back . . . go back to the past, to the senseless waiting, to life with our luggage packed. Our dream of living in Israel was incomparably stronger than fear of the suffering we might be made to endure.

By going away we would not have harmed anybody.

I wanted to live over there with my family, work there. I would not have bothered about politics—all my interest in politics has been confined to the simple wish to leave. Even now I do not doubt for a minute that some time I shall go after all and that I *will* live in Israel. . . . This dream, illuminated by two thousand years of hope, will never leave me. NEXT YEAR IN JERUSALEM! And now I repeat:

> *"if I forget you, Oh, Jerusalem*
> *let my right hand wither away. . . ."*
> *"Im eshkacheich Yerusalayim,*
> *tishkach yemini et kochi. . . ."*

THE EDUCATION TAX

Since late in 1970, all Jews leaving the Soviet Union have been charged a basic fee of $550 to renounce their Soviet citizenship, plus $450 in passport charges (a total of 900 Rubles).

In addition to these costs, in the summer of 1972, the Soviet government adopted a new regulation which added additional exit taxes and fees to would-be emigrants with advanced education degrees. In those cases where the tax has been invoked, charges have been as follows: High School graduate—$6,750. Medical Doctor—$10,500. Engineer—$9,625. Research Scientist—$22,000. Professor—$23,750. Apparently the tax has been implemented on a selective, and seemingly arbitrary, basis.

Many motivations have been suggested for the imposition of the education tax. Some believe that the government is continuing its policy aimed at harassing and intimidating potential immigrants to Israel. Others contend that the Soviet authorities are acting more out of national self-interest. In this view, the government has acted to stop the "brain drain" of skilled Jewish technicians and professionals to foreign countries. Also, in the past few years other nationalities in the USSR, in addition to the Jews, have become increasingly militant. Therefore the State is seeking, by the tax and other measures, to stop the ferment among the minorities, beginning with the Jews, and is attempting to reassert its authority and discipline. All would agree, however, that the Jewish nationality is the one most affected by the new law.

The following is the text of the regulation as adopted by the Presidium of the Supreme Soviet and the Council of Ministers of the USSR on August 3, 1972, and put into effect on August 14.

>Law 572. Citizens of the USSR leaving for permanent residence abroad in other than Socialist countries are under obligation to compensate the State for their education received from institutions of higher learning, for graduate work, medical internships, graduate military service, and for receiving the respective academic degrees.
>
>Law 573. The Council of Ministers of the USSR adopts and affirms the Decree 572 of the Supreme Soviet and directs the Ministries of Finance and Higher Education to institute education fees as compensation for the expenditures for education in institutions of higher learning for persons departing for permanent residence in capitalist countries, and also authorizes the organization of the Ministries of Finance and Internal Affairs to grant in exceptional cases partial or full exemption from payment of these fees.

1. What was the extent of the public reaction which responded to the trials and the tax? How did Communist Parties in the West (Italy and France) react? How did the United States government and Congress respond? How would you measure the effectiveness of this response?
2. If you were the Soviet prosecutor in the Leningrad trial, how would you present the case for the Soviet government? If you were a Jewish defendant, how would you respond?
3. If you were a Soviet Jew and wished to assimilate and to remain in the USSR, how might these two developments affect your life and future? Is it easier for a Jew to assimilate in the United States or in the USSR?
4. What is the fate of Silva Zalmanson and other Soviet

Jewish prisoners? How can we help to aid them in their present condition?

5. In what other ways are Soviet Jews harassed and intimidated when they have made known their desire to emigrate to Israel?

6. If you were a Soviet Jew living in Moscow, how much tax could your family be required to pay the government to leave the USSR?

7. The Jewish people has been under the threat of ransom tax in earlier periods in Jewish history. How did the Jewish community then respond? How should we respond?

RUSSIAN JEWISH EMIGRATION

In 1971, a long hoped for, but virtually unexpected development took place regarding the relationship of the Soviet government to some of the Jews of the USSR. An emigration of unprecedented proportion left the Soviet Union for *aliyah* to Israel. The number was the largest legal exit of Soviet citizens in the 54-year history of the Soviet regime. All of the emigrants left with official permission and carried proper visa and travel documents. The entire spectrum of economic levels, social strata, professional background and political affiliation was represented, in addition to a wide age and geographic distribution. The reasons behind such a Soviet move are only subject to speculation.

The following article is reprinted from the Israeli daily *Ma'ariv* of January 5, 1972.

IN 1971 13,905 PEOPLE CAME TO ISRAEL FROM THE U.S.S.R.

By Harry Trimborn
L.A. Times Correspondent in Moscow

Thirteen thousand nine hundred and five Soviet Jews immigrated to Israel during 1971. The pace of the *aliyah* increased in the final quarter of the year, and apparently will continue also in the current year, according to reliable sources in Moscow.

This is an unprecedented exit in the 54-year history of the Soviet Union. This is the first time that such a large group of Soviet citizens (with whose exit they were obligated to renounce their citizenship) left the state in a planned fashion, by means of legal emigration.

Nevertheless, the number of those leaving is only a tiny fraction of the 2.2 million Jews residing in the Soviet Union according to the official census—and no one knows the number of those wishing to leave.

The wave of *aliyah* from the Soviet Union in 1971 ended with a strange innovation: the disinterment of Jewish graves for the reburial of the remains in Israel.

A special transport plane of the Soviet airline "Aeroflot" left the day before yesterday en route to Vienna, the major crossroads for Soviet Jewish emigration, containing the coffin of a Jew for shipment to Israel. According to the reports from completely reliable sources, until now the remains of approximately one dozen dead have been transferred from cemeteries in the Soviet Union for burial in Israel.

There have also been a number of cases of elderly immigrants from Soviet Georgia, and from other places in the Soviet Union, who died on their way to Israel, in Moscow or Vienna, and whose remains were brought to Israel by members of the families.

On Monday, January 3rd, the first work day of 1972, the Soviet authorities issued 210 visa permits to Soviet citizens. This is a single day's record, and the number does not include children under the age of 15, who are included in the visa permits of their parents or guardians.

1971's total number of emigrants was 14-times greater than the number leaving in 1970, and was 3,500 people greater than the 10,330 Soviet Jews who immigrated to Israel in the ten year period 1961-1970.

The Soviet authorities continued to claim that only a handful of elderly, disabled, and children are leaving. In reality, Soviet citizens of all ages, from all strata of society, and from all walks of life are leaving.

These have included scientists and doctors, workers and

merchants, musicians and film producers, agricultural workers and construction men. Political and religious activists who strongly object to the suppression of civil and political freedoms by the Kremlin, and to the efforts of the regime to prevent the Jews from living according to the cultural and religious traditions of their ancestors, have also been among those who have been allowed to depart.

Among the Jews who left, many had no particular political, cultural or social motive for doing so. These—perhaps a majority of the immigrants—left the Soviet Union for the same reasons that moved waves of Swedes, Germans, Irish, and other nationalities to cross the Atlantic Ocean in the 19th century and at the start of the 20th century, in order to take part in the building of America: economic possibilities.

With the exception of the political and religious activists, who are a minority among the emigrants, it seems from various surveys that many of the Jews did not feel themselves particularly deprived by the authorities because of their Jewishness. This in particular applies to the Georgians.

The political and religious activists came mainly from the Baltic Republics (Latvia, Lithuania, and Estonia). In this area latent and, at times, overt nationalism exists, with particular bitterness at the fact that prior to the Second World War these republics were forcibly annexed to the Soviet Union.

The remainder of those leaving are from Moscow, and from various urban centers in the European portion of the Soviet Union.

Apparently the Soviet intention is to rebuild in part the influence of Moscow on Israel which collapsed with the breaking of diplomatic relations following the Six Day War. The Soviet Union was among the first powers to recognize the State of Israel in 1948, and in spite of the Soviet Union's anti-Semitic past, there exists a strong Jewish influence in the Bolshevik revolutionary tradition. Many of the Israeli leaders and citizens come from Russia, and in spite of the present political differences, there exists in Isreal a latent affection for Russia. The severing of relations between the two countries was seen as a tragedy, inconsistent with the policies of the great powers.

It is possible that the Soviet Union is attempting to avail herself of these feelings in her allowing *aliyah* of noticeable proportions, even while not restoring diplomatic relations.

Questions to Consider

1. What was the total number of Russian Jews coming to Israel from 1961 through 1971? How many have come since?

2. How does this article explain this marked increase in *aliyah*? How would you account for it? Why does the Soviet government allow this Russian Jewish emigration?

3. Which Soviet Jews would like to emigrate but are currently not allowed? What do you know about them and their plight? For what reasons are they not allowed to leave?

4. How many Russian Jews do you believe would wish to come to Israel to live? How would you arrive at a responsible guess?

5. Which other national-ethnic groups (*Eydot*) have come to Israel since 1948? What aspects of their culture and customs did they transplant to Israel? How will the Russian Jews integrate into Israeli life?

6. What will the effect of these immigrants be on Israeli society? What problems of immigration and absorption will their coming create? How can American Jews help to alleviate their problems?

7. What was the total number of American Jews coming to Israel since 1948, and particularly in the last decade?

8. Why don't more American Jews want to move to Israel? Do you? Why or why not?

A MODEL JEWISH COMMUNITY

Assignment

A group of Jewish businessmen and financiers has just banded together, purchased a plot of land, and plans to move thousands of Jews there. For this project money is no object.

You are in charge of constructing a model Jewish community whose goal is producing an active and meaningful Jewish environment and life.

What institutions and community organizations would you create and want to include in such a model community? Include minimally the following areas: religious, social, cultural.

As aids, refer to city maps of past and present flourishing Jewish communities, as Vilna and Jerusalem, if they are available. Your local telephone directory under the headings "Jewish" or "Hebrew" might also offer some direction.

A special meeting of the backers will be held in the very near future. You will then be asked to present your findings and the results of your research. You can actually help shape the future American Jewish community.

THE RUSSIAN JEWISH COMMUNITY

Realizing that the status of Jewish life in the Soviet Union is remote from the ideal, it is still useful to have a standard with which to compare it. In the following exercise compare your model of a Jewish community with the current status of such Jewish institutions in the Soviet Union.

For current information on the status of Jewish institutions and life in the USSR, consult your local Soviet Jewry Committee, the National Jewish Community Relations Advisory Council (55 West 42nd Street, New York, N. Y. 10036), or the National Conference on Soviet Jews (11 West 55th Street, New York City 10036). The National Conference publishes a "Fact Sheet on Soviet Jewry."

INSTITUTION   STATUS FOR SOVIET JEWS

I. *Religious*
   Mikvah (for example)

II. *Social*
    Jewish Youth Organization

INSTITUTION   STATUS FOR SOVIET JEWS

III. *Cultural*
Jewish Museum

IV. *Other*
Jewish Teacher's Seminary

Questions to Consider

1. How does your local Jewish community compare with the model you have constructed?
2. What are the weaknesses and strengths of your local Jewish community?
3. How can young Jews help to improve the local Jewish community and communal life, and to make it more meaningful?
4. Summarize the major areas of concern in the contemporary condition of the Jewish community in the Soviet Union.

CLASS TRIP TO THE SOVIET UNION

Let's go to Russia! Travel to the Soviet Union for American Jewish tourists involves a number of technical arrangements, and has a special moral dimension. The following is an outline for planning a trip to the Soviet Union, especially designed for a teenage and adult Jewish group.

To answer the appropriate questions and problems, refer to diaries of trips to Russia, and invite a guest traveler to share his experiences. Discuss the visit with a local travel agent. *The Jewish Travel Guide, The Travelers Guide to Jewish Landmarks of Europe* and *The Briefing Kit For Travelers to the USSR* (see bibliography) should be consulted.

1. *To Go or Not to Go*

Why should Jews travel to the Soviet Union? What can one hope to accomplish by a visit? Won't there be plenty of other tourists going who could do the task just as well?

How does one answer those who refuse to travel to the Soviet Union out of a desire not to support the economy of a Communist country?

2. *Itinerary*

When is the most convenient time to go? What are the costs of a trip to Russia? How much difference in price is there between going in the on-season and the off-season?

Which Soviet cities should be included in the trip? On what basis does one choose an itinerary?

How much time, due to the cost and travel factors, should be spent in the Soviet Union? What sources of information could be consulted to find out the Soviet airline and train schedules? How is it possible to avoid intra-city travel on Shabbat? How can Shabbat travel between cities be avoided?

What sources of information could be consulted to find out the time of Shabbat in various Russian cities?

3. *Travel Documents*

What is the projected cost of the trip?

What is "Intourist?" What is the procedure for getting a visa to the Soviet Union? How much time will it take and what will it cost? How does one go about getting a United States Passport? When are plane reservations made?

4. *Pre-Travel Preparations—What to Bring*

What kinds of clothing should one bring for a Russian trip?

What types of "gifts" should a Jewish traveler bring to Russia, if any? What are some of the moral considerations involved in this decision? What has been the Soviet government's policy in this regard?

What are the *Kashrut* facilities in Russia? Would any special foods have to be brought along?

What types of articles and documents should *not* be brought into the Soviet Union?

5. *Pre-Travel Preparations—What to Study*

What foreign language preparation should be made prior to the trip? Is it worthwhile learning the Russian alphabet? What use could be made of this knowledge?

Which fields of Jewish interest should be reviewed? What

kinds of questions or requests might be made by Russians or Russian Jews, for which travelers should be prepared?

What sources would one consult to locate Jewish sites and landmarks in each city on the itinerary?

6. *Arrival in the Soviet Union*

How much freedom do tourists have in Russia? When are visitors allowed to be without a guide? Should one visit the United States Embassy in Moscow? Is there anyone connected with the Embassy who should be consulted in particular? How should one act so as not to be charged with being "provocative" or "propagandistic?" Are there spies and microphones watching tourists? Is it permissible to keep a diary? What kinds of notations should not be made?

What kinds of things should definitely *not* be done on a trip to the Soviet Union?

7. *Relations with Jews*

Where are the best places to meet Soviet Jews? How can one go "fishing" for Jews? Should tourists wear or carry any outward signs of Jewishness?

Where might a tourist expect to meet the following Jews? What kinds of questions might these Jews ask? What reactions might they have towards visiting American Jews? What kinds of questions should be asked of them?

- a 66-year-old pensioner, born in Poland
- a 20-year-old student at the University of Moscow, from Riga, Latvia
- a 29-year-old engineer in a hydro-electric plant
- his wife and 4-year-old daughter
- an avowedly pro-Soviet student of foreign languages, born in Moscow

a teacher of Hebrew in a foreign language institute
a teenage member of the Soviet Jewish underground
a *Sefardi shochet* who once studied in the Moscow Yeshivah
a *gabbai* employed by the Soviet government
the editor of *Sovetish Heymland*
the Chief Rabbi of Moscow
a 17-year-old high school student

To which of these Jews might one want to leave gifts? How does a tourist transfer the gift to them? What are the moral dimensions of giving gifts to Soviet Jews?

8. *Things to Look for*

In what ways could prospective Jewish travelers prepare themselves to be as sensitive as possible to the condition of Jewish life in the USSR? What insights could be gained from the following:

a visit to the *Dom Kniga*, the largest bookstore in Leningrad?
the listing of evening performances in the Intourist office?
the inside of a synagogue when no services are going on?
the exterior and locations of the synagogue?
the Rembrandt collection at the Hermitage Museum in Leningrad?
the collection of World War II paintings at the Tretyakov Art Gallery in Moscow?
the Institute of Near East studies in Leningrad?
the birthplace of Shalom Aleichem?
the Museum of Religion and Atheism in Leningrad?
the card catalogues of the Lenin State Library in Moscow?

What other examples can you suggest?

What kind of a picture can one hope to get of the situation of Jewish life in the Soviet Union from one short visit?

9. *Returning Home*

What are the moral dimensions involved in having been to the Soviet Union? What should be told others about what has been seen and experienced? What kind of programs could a returning traveler sponsor or conduct? What kind of information should not be publicized?

Assignment: Divide into committees for each of the Soviet cities on the class itinerary, and prepare a report which should include minimally the following information about the particular city:

   a. its brief general history;
   b. its Jewish history and Jewish significance;
   c. Jewish and non-Jewish population statistics;
   d. Jewish sites and their addresses;
   e. sites of general interest and importance;
   f. their location on a map of the city;
   g. particular problems of Jewish travellers there;
   h. the situation of Jews in the city;
   i. your suggestions for a day-by-day itinerary.

Sources consulted could include high school history textbooks, the *Time-Life* series on Russia, as well as the Jewish travellers' guides noted above, reports from tourists, and guide books to the Soviet Union published by the Soviet authorities. Slides and photographs should also be consulted and shared with the class.

AFTERWARD

In the final analysis, we are still thousands of miles away from the Jews of the Soviet Union. Although this textbook and study has endeavored to bring ourselves nearer to their history, spirit, and ways of living, the distance remains great.

This book can serve as a guide into the past and present, but it can not anticipate or predict the future. Almost everyone who has studied the problem of Soviet Jewry in depth forms his own view of what the future will bring. In your opinion, and judging by world events when reading this "Afterward," what is to be the future fate of Soviet Jewry?

Will they continue to rise up and clamor for emigration to Israel and the West? Will a spirit of passivity and docility develop, making them fearful of any protest? Will the authorities answer with an additional wave of arrests, trials, and repression, and totally frustrate any independent action? Will the Jewish militant leadership be allowed to leave, leaving Soviet Jewry leaderless? Will Israel prove to be the homeland that the Soviet Jews believed it would be? How will those permitted to emigrate be absorbed into Israeli life and society? Will the future mood of the youth and their parents be one of hope and patience, or of fear and depression?

How could you apply the lessons discussed from Tsarist and Soviet Jewish history in attempting an analysis and solution of these problems? What role will American Jewry play in the future of Soviet Jewry?

In Moscow on *Simchat Torah*, the Jewish youth sing "*Ahm Yisrael Chai*"—"The Jewish People continues to live." Will their children sing it 20 years hence?

Appendix

INTRODUCTION

The Appendix is divided into two sections. The first, entitled "Projects and Activities," is designed to supplement the classroom discussions and study with different educational formats. For convenience these activities are divided into three categories: I. Classroom Learning Projects; II. Community Educating Projects; III. Community Activating Projects.

The first suggestions, including the study of the Russian and Yiddish languages, map and genealogical work, role-playing and dramatization, are aimed at enriching the classroom learning experience. The second group includes projects directed outside the classroom into the youth and adult communities. The creation of educational materials and programs, and the involvement of the synagogue, the home, and the public school are stressed. The third section focuses around activating members of the class and the community to widely express and publicize their concern for the problem of Soviet Jewry. Political action and making contact with Soviet Jews is emphasized.

Since these projects and activities are planned to enhance and to expand the formal classroom discussions, they should be implemented concurrently with the regular study units.

The second half of the Appendix, entitled "Self Test Review," surveys much of the factual material presented in this text book. It can be either assigned as homework, or done together as a class. An answer sheet has been provided at the end.

PROJECTS AND REVIEW

I. Classroom Learning Projects

1. Learn how to read the Russian alphabet. The exercises in *Fundamentals of Russian*, Horace G. Hunt (W. W. Norton and Co., New York, 1958, pages 25-27) are particularly useful, but any Russian language text or pocket book will suffice.

This skill can be used in studying maps from the Tsarist and Soviet periods, in reading placards and signs from the press, and in following Russian literature in dual-language translations.

For example, only a rudimentary reading knowledge of Russian is required to follow a recording of Yevgeny Yettushenko reading from "Babi Yar" (Caedmon Records TC 1153, 505 Eighth Avenue, New York City 10018).

2. Prepare a family genealogy for your own family, going back at least four generations. Focus on the original and maiden names, places of residence, dates of birth and death, and periods of emigration.

Locate your family town on a map of Tsarist Russia. Involve your parents and other relatives in your search for the appropriate information.

3. Familiarize yourself with a "Jewish map of the Tsarist Empire and of Soviet Russia. Locate the following:

> The borders of the Pale of Settlement (approximately Vitebsk to Lodz, and south of Riga to Odessa).

Major non-Jewish cities of Western Russia (St. Petersburg/Leningrad, Moscow, Kiev).
Centers of Jewish cultural and industrial life (Vilna, Kovno, Riga, Bialystok, Minsk).
Centers of *Haskalah* and Jewish publishing (Warsaw, Odessa, Grodno, Zhitomer).
Homes of famous Yeshivot (Slobodka, Volozhin, Mir, Telshe, Ponovitch).
Chassidic centers (Lubovitch, Lyady, Mogilev, Berditchev, Bratslev).
Sephardic Jewish communities (Tbilisi, Kutaisi, Samarkand, Bukhara).

4. Learn how to read and speak Yiddish. *College Yiddish* by Uriel Weinreich (YIVO, New York, 1949) is the finest Yiddish text available. Also study the derivations and meanings of commonly used American Yiddish phrases. There are a number of popular books on this topic.

Read the literature of the great 19th century Yiddish writers in translation, including Shalom Aleichem.

5. Leave the classroom to take advantage of movies relating to the Jewish experience in Russia (*The Fixer*), the Shoah (*The Pawnbroker, Judgement at Nuremberg, Night and Fog, Let My People Go*), and to the non-Jewish environment surrounding the Russian Jew (*War and Peace, Dr. Zhivago, Nicholas and Alexandra*).

6. Contact Simeon Weisenthal, Documentation Center, Rudolfsplatz 7/III, Vienna 1010 Austria, concerning aiding in his search for Nazi war criminals still at large. He is also engaged in documenting contemporary manifestations of anti-Semitism in the Soviet Union and Eastern Europe.

7. Dramatize Russian Jewish literature in the form of

plays, dramatic readings, the dance, and other creative expressions.

Short stories by Isaac Babel, Yevtushenko's "Babi Yar," and the tales of Shalom Aleichem particularly lend themselves to adaptations. Scripts are available from "The Eternal Light" radio program (c/o 3080 Broadway, New York City).

8. Dramatize historical scenes and dialogues relating to the Jews of Russia. For example:

If Israel Lost the War (Coward McCann, New York City, 1969) by Richard Chesnoff and others, pages 90-101, reconstructs a discussion held in the Kremlin in June, 1967, as to whether the Soviet Union should support Egypt in the Six-Day War. Although the account is a creation of the author's imagination, it concretizes the inner workings of the Soviet government regarding Israel and the Middle East.

Prologue to Revolution (Prentice-Hall, New Jersey, 1967) by Professor Michael Cherniavsky, pages 56-64, 85-86, records the actual minutes of the discussions of a secret meeting of the Tsarist Council of Ministers in 1915. The major topic is whether the Pale of Settlement should be abolished, and what the consequences of this act would be for the Russian people and the Jews. A full spectrum of opinions current in the Tsarist court is quoted, ranging from extreme liberal to rabid anti-Semite.

9. Assign one student the role of a Soviet official visiting your classroom. He should familiarize himself with the current Soviet position, logic, and rhetoric. Engage him in a discussion and see which of you constructs a more convincing argument.

II. Community Educating Projects

1. Collect news items from the Anglo-Jewish press, *The Jewish Chronicle* from London, *The Jerusalem Post*, the Jew-

ish Telegraphic Agency, and local newspapers and magazines, and display them in the classroom, the school building, and the main congregational facility.

2. Publish a periodical featuring Soviet Jewry and *K'lal Yisrael*, and include material covered in classroom discussions and sessions.

3. Research and write articles for national Jewish youth publications (those sponsored by USY, NFTY, NCSY, BBYO, and the Zionist movements), your synagogue bulletin, and local Jewish papers.

Write a series of articles for your local public school newspapers.

4. Collect and catalogue a library of 35 mm. slides on the topic of Russian and Soviet Jewry for presentations and assemblies.

5. Interview travellers to the USSR and collect their impressions for a "Travellers Diary" of information.

Prepare a memo for tourists planning to travel to the Soviet Union, including the location of Jewish places of interest (synagogues, monuments, cemeteries), directions how to find them, histories of various Jewish communities, and current Soviet Jewry information. *The Travellers Guide to Jewish Landmarks of Europe* by Postal and Abramson and *The Briefing Kit for Travellers to the USSR* by Baum and Furst (see bibliography for information) are invaluable.

Circulate these memos through local travel agents, or by going directly to major international airports (such as New York's JFK) and seeking out travellers on their way to the Soviet Union.

6. Plan to travel to the Soviet Union yourself with Jewish youth groups or other tours. Contact Soviet Jewry offices prior to leaving, for proper orientation. Maintaining live con-

tact with Jews of the free world is essential for the continued life of Soviet Jewry.

7. Prepare a "Soviet Jewry Kit" including a fact sheet, letters of protest from Soviet Jews, maps of historical and contemporary interest, and suggestions for action, for use in conventions, and for the homes of synagogue members.

8. Create new formats for presenting the theme of Soviet Jewry, including mixed media, slide and tape productions, movies, filmstrips, and collages.

9. Involve other classrooms of the Hebrew school, Hebrew high school, sisterhood, and men's club. Serve as the teacher to other students and adults.

Conduct a school assembly on special occasions, as on the *Yahrtzeit* of important Russian Jewish personalities, or to alert the student body to critical situations.

10. Increasing numbers of public high schools are offering Free Universities in addition to the regular curriculum of of classes. Establish a course on Soviet Jewry within this framework. Formulate your own mini-course lasting 3-5 sessions (or more) on the major problems and hopes of Soviet Jews. Use this textbook as a source for materials.

11. Compose prayers and other religious formats on behalf of Soviet Jewry. The Chief Rabbinate of Israel (c/o Heichal Shlomo, Jerusalem) and your local Rabbi will be of guidance. Incorporate them into youth services or regular synagogue worship.

The National Conference on Soviet Jewry (11 West 42nd Street, New York City 10036) has issued a prayer for the *Pesach Seder* entitled, "This is the Matzah of Hope." The English text follows (for Hebrew and Yiddish versions contact the National Conference).

THIS IS THE MATZAH OF HOPE

This *matzah* which we set aside as a symbol of hope for the Jews in the Soviet Union, reminds us of the indestructible links that exist between us.

As we observe this festival of freedom, we know that Soviet Jews are not free to leave without harassment; to learn of their past; to pass on their religious traditions; to learn the language of their fathers; to train the teachers and the rabbis of future generations.

We remember with bitterness the scores of Jewish prisoners of conscience who sought to live as Jews and struggle to leave for Israel—the land of our fathers—but now languish in bondage in Soviet labor camps. Their struggle against their oppressors is part of an ongoing effort, and they shall know that they have not been forgotten.

As Soviet Jews assert themselves they are joined by all who are aroused by their affliction.

We will continue until they emerge into the light of freedom.

12. Design symbols of the Jewish community in the USSR and publicize them. These could include letter seals, posters, and an original flag of the Jewish nationality (perhaps a yellow *Menorah* or *Magen David* on a field of red).

13. Order stickers or rubber stamps with the legend "Remember Soviet Jews" for use on personal, organizational, and synagogue mail. Design the stamp with the message in English, Hebrew, and Russian.

14. Contact the history department of your local high school and arrange for programs and speakers on Soviet Jewry.

Feature the theme of Soviet Jewry in your term papers, book reports, and other public school presentations.

15. Compose and teach appropriate songs of Soviet Jews.

Utilize newly released records of conversations with Soviet Jews, and of songs and presentations on their behalf. Of special note are "The New Slavery" (AME records, 185 West End Ave., New York City 10023) with interviews of Soviet Jews in Moscow, and "Silent No More" (Star Record Company, 520 Fifth Avenue, New York City 10036) sung and narrated by Theodore Bikel, based on tapes smuggled out of the USSR.

16. Invite a past participant in the United Synagogue Youth Eastern European Pilgrimage to speak and share his experiences. Names are available from: United Synagogue Youth, 218 East 70th St., New York City 10021.

17. Subscribe to one of the Russian language newspapers published in Israel ("Tribuna," Rechov Herzel 113, Tel Aviv). The stories will provide information about emerging cultural and communal institutions among the Russian Jewish immigrants in Israel.

III. COMMUNITY ACTIVATING PROJECTS

1. Participate in and sponsor rallies and protests in support of Soviet Jews. Keep in mind that such meetings are only one form of action on behalf of Soviet Jewry.

2. Conduct a teach-in or an all-night vigil for Soviet Jewry. These can be linked to traditional Jewish forms of expression, as a *Tikkun Leil Shavuot*, or an all night *Pesach Seder* program.

3. Place advertisements in newspapers concerning the situation of Soviet Jews, particularly during the period of Jewish holidays. Invite adults in the congregation to sponsor such ads in the names of their businesses.

4. Write letters-to-the-editor of local and school newspapers. Encourage Jewish and non-Jewish friends to do likewise.

5. Conduct a letter writing campaign on behalf of Soviet Jewry. Direct correspondence to high United States public officials including your congressman (c/o House Office Building, Washington, D. C.) your senators (c/o Senate Office Building, Washington, D. C.), and the President (The White House, Washington, D. C.).

Relate specifically to the current Soviet Jewish situation, urge the issuing of public statements, press for congressional legislation to bring pressure on the Soviet government, and request that the topic of Soviet Jewry be placed on the official agenda for top level United States-Soviet meetings.

6. Begin a chain letter on behalf of Soviet Jews.

7. Collect signatures on petitions demanding the improvement in the status on Soviet Jews, and allowing *aliyah* to Israel for those who wish.

Xerox copies of petitions sent to Soviet officials, and forward them to the Human Rights Commission, United Nations, New York City 10017. Request a written acknowledgment. All complaints of violations of human rights must be recorded by the Human Rights Commission and circulated to member states of the United Nations.

8. A Political Action Message telegram can be sent through Western Union for a nominal charge. Send telegrams to American public officials, and to Soviet governmental officials based in the United States.

9. Send mail to the Soviet Union for the Jewish holidays, especially for *Pesach* and *Rosh Hashanah*.

Design your own greeting cards with the aid of someone with a knowledge of Russian, Hebrew, and Yiddish. Keep the messages non-political and encouraging. Local Soviet Jewry councils have also produced their own greeting cards.

Soviet Jews publicize their names to keep themselves in the public eye, and thereby secure a measure of protection from the Soviet authorities. Do not let their risk be in vain.

10. Write to families of arrested and imprisoned Soviet Jews. Convey your prayers and encouragement.

Addresses can be obtained from local Soviet Jewry councils.

Under international postal regulations, registered letters must be delivered, otherwise the foreign governmental postal system has to pay a fine. To insure delivery, send your letters by registered mail.

11. Write directly to prisoners held in Soviet jails and prison camps, and forward complaints to the American Red Cross, the International Red Cross, and the Voice for Universal Rights.

Request neutral foreign observers to inspect the prison facilities.

Some addresses include: George Elsey, President, American Red Cross, 2025 E. Street, N.W., Washington, D. C. 20006; Heinrik Beer, Secretary General, League of Red Cross Societies, Petit Saconner, Geneva, Switzerland; Marcel Naville, President, International Committee of the Red Cross, 7 Avenue de la Paix, Geneva, Switzerland.

12. Telephone activist Soviet Jews directly. Some speak English and Hebrew in addition to Russian. Costs are about $12.00 for three minutes.

Contact your local Soviet Jewish organization, the Community Relations Council of Federation, the National Conference for Soviet Jewry, or the National Jewish Community Relations Advisory Council for details.

13. Pledge to "adopt" a Soviet Jew with the following actions:

    a. writing a letter to him monthly and on Jewish holidays,

b. communicating often with your congressman and senator,

c. trying to involve new people in the area of Soviet Jewry,

d. participating in rallies and other programs on behalf of Soviet Jewry.

Upon receipt of the "pledge" to adopt a Soviet Jew, the coordinating committee forwards the name of his "adopted" Soviet Jew.

14. Cable Soviet officials directly conveying your concern, including: The Premier of the Soviet Union and the First Secretary of the Communist Party (Kremlin, Moscow, RSFSR, USSR), and the Prosecutor-General of the Soviet Union (Pushkinskaya 15 A, Moscow, RSFSR, USSR).

15. The United H.I.A.S. Service (200 Park Avenue South, New York City, New York 10003, (212) 674-6800) had developed procedures for reuniting Jews in the Soviet Union with their relatives in the free world. The procedures include issuing of "letters of invitation," proper translations, labor certificates, and passport and visa costs, are all outlined and detailed in H.I.A.S. information memos.

Contact them if you know of American families who maintain contact with relatives in the Soviet Union. Contact as well local branches of H.I.A.S. in your community through the Federations and Jewish Family Service agencies.

16. Keep in weekly contact with Soviet Jewry "Hotlines" throughout the country. Lines have been established in New York, Chicago, Los Angeles, Miami, and Baltimore, among others. Contact the local Soviet Jewry Committee for information.

If none exists, set up a Soviet Hot Line in your community. Utilize a telephone answering service machine to give a brief message on the latest situation in the USSR and your community. Ask local politicians and community leaders to record the message, publicize the number in periodicals, and make small Hot Line stickers to attach to telephones with the phone number.

17. Join the Student Struggle for Soviet Jewry (200 West 72nd Street, New York City 10023), and encourage your parents to support the Center for Russian Jewry at the same address. Special student memberships are available.

18. Organize local area conferences of Soviet Jewry, or support the ones already existing in your area.

For up-to-date information concerning Soviet Jewry projects, contact the following: The National Conference on Soviet Jewry (11 West 55th Street, New York City, N. Y. 10036), the National Jewish Community Relations Advisory Council (55 West 42nd Street, New York City 10036), the Academic Committee on Soviet Jewry (315 Lexington Avenue, New York City 10816), Jewish Minorities Research and Conference on the Status of Soviet Jews (16 East 85th Street, New York City, N. Y. 10028) and the American Jewish Committee (165 East 56th Street, New York, N. Y.), among others.

19. Plant a tree in Israel in the forest of honor of Jews of the Soviet Union. Contact the Jewish National Fund (42 East 59th Street, New York, N. Y. 10021) for information. The cost is $2.50 per tree.

Forward the certificate directly to Jews in the Soviet Union.

In addition to encouraging the Soviet Jews, this would also be fulfilling the *Mitzvah* of rebuilding and resettling the land of Israel.

The following program techniques might be helpful:

20. Recreate a Soviet synagogue scene in your home congregation.

In conjunction with your rabbi, arrange for services to be held without *Siddurim* or *Tallitot*, and with "officials" of the government present. Include a prayer for the government of the Soviet Union, and have a Soviet flag present in the sanctuary.

21. Close and lock the doors of the synagogue before the congregants gather, and post the following sign: "Synagogue closed by the authorities for anti-State behavior."

22. Enter a congregational or board meeting and declare all the participants under arrest "for teaching religious propaganda and Zionism." After the initial shock has worn off, have a discussion on the status of communal life in the Soviet Union and in the United States.

23. Chain the wrists of a student together with bicycle chains, mask his lips with red tape, place a *Magen David* on his back, and have him walk in a public place (shopping center, school yard).

Someone should follow him handing out circulars explaining that the Jews of the free world have to be the voice of silenced Soviet Jewry.

24. On the occasion of Soviet cultural exchanges and presentations in the United States, hand out programs welcoming the visitors in the name of world peace, but reminding the audience that Soviet Jews still do not have their national and cultural rights.

25. Project lifesize a 35mm. slide photograph of a synagogue scene in the Soviet Union. Arrange for a student to step out of the screen, and to share the experience of Soviet Jews.

SELF-TEST REVIEW

This self-test review is designed to integrate various aspects of the history and contemporary situation of the Russian and Soviet Jewish community, and to review much of the material examined in this textbook.

Fill in the blanks with the correct answer (usually only a number, date, or a single word). Consult Baron for additional information and answers.

THE RUSSIAN JEWISH COMMUNITY

Although the vast majority of Jews did not come to Eastern Europe until the .... (1) centuries, there existed a semi-legendary, semi-factual settlement of Jews near the .... (2) Sea, by the name of the .... (3).

The modern settlement of Jews in Eastern Europe came as a result of the expulsions, first from .... (4), then .... (5), and finally from .... (6), the immediate neighbor of the Polish Kingdom. Economically the Jews served the Polish great landowners and the Crown. Their community authority, the .... (7), had wide powers. The highest communal status was reserved for those who excelled in .... (8). The Jews of Poland had an independent status, and were secure. This came to an abrupt end with the period of the pogroms led by the Cossack Hetman .... (9) in the years .... (10), known in Hebrew as .... (11). The toll was fearsome. The world Jewish population declined, according to some estimates, to only .... (12) people, the lowest in Jewish history. The economic basis of the community was ruined, its political and religious status were undermined, and a sense of foreboding was rampant. Into this gap came a rash of false .... (13), notably the most successful and most widely received of them all, ... (14). With their unmasking, an indigenous religious Jewish reaction developed, preaching hope to the masses in south Russia, called .... (15). Its first great leader was called the .... (16). Their antagonists were known as the .... (17), and were led by the Gaon Rabbi Elijah from the town of .... (18).

Eastern European Jewry became part of the Russian Empire with the partitions of .... (19), in 17.., 17.., and 17.. (20). Russia received an unwanted million Jews, and the Jews found themselves unwittingly a part of the Tsarist Empire. Although politically oppressed, they retained spiritual autonomy. This was due in great part to the Tsarist policy of confining the Jews to one part of the country, called, the .... of .... (21). At times, the Jews of the region were faced with the choice between the physically restrictive policy of the Tsar or the enlightened life of the West. This most notably occurred in the reaction of Rabbi Shneur Zalman from Lyadi to the invasion of .... (22) in the year .... (23).

With the 19th century, there were a number of attempts to further restrict the spiritual life of the Jews, notably the Crown Schools and "Khappers" of the reign of Tsar .... (24). His policy of "Orthodoxy, Autocracy, and Nationalism" did not succeed. Instead, 19th century Russian Jewry became the population pool for world Jewry.

Unfortunately, the restrictions did not stop, and the poverty and pogroms left .... (25) as the only escape for millions of East European Jews. The United States of America became the newfound homeland for the vast majority of them.

Those millions who remained (the Tsarist census at the end of the 19th century lists nearly .... (26) million Jews in Russia) looked for other solutions to their plight. Some answers took Jewish nationalist forms, as .... (27), while others joined with the workers of the world, as the members of the .... (28) parties. Many of the early Communist Party leaders were Russian Jews, notably the Chief Commissary of Lenin's Red Army .... (29), whose Jewish name had been Lev Davidovitch Bronstein. Many leaders of the State of Israel were Russian Jews, including all of the Prime Ministers: .... (30) named Greene in Russia, ... (31) named Shertok, ... (32) named Shkolnik, and .... (33) named Meyerson.

The turn of the century evidenced only further degradations. Two outstanding examples which shocked world opinion were the pogrom of 1903 in the city of .... (34), and the .... (35) Case, where the lie of the blood libel was revived.

Only with the Russian Revolution in the month of .... (36), 1917, were the Jewish disabilities removed, and even this was only temporary until the Bolshevik Revolution in the month of .... (37), 1917.

With the new Communist government, the Jewish policies and fate took a new turn. The Jewish Sections of the Communist Party, called the .... (38), took an active anti-Zionist and anti-religious stand. Hebrew publications were cut off. The economic position of the Jews was .... (39). However, the Jewish nationality was allowed to use its official language .... (40). An attempt was even made to organize a Jewish homeland within the Soviet Union called .... (41). The friendship pact signed in 1939 between the .... (42) and .... (43) signalled a new freeze on the Jewish position in the Soviet Union. This was added to the already depleted situation of the Jewish leadership following the famous Purge Trials of the 1930's. The Fourth Partition of .... (44) in 1939 brought into the Soviet orbit many millions of non-Sovietized Jews who, under normal conditions, would have been forced into the Soviet mold. Only World War II brought a short respite in the name of national unity.

During the War, with the attack of Germany on the Soviet Union in ...., 19.. (45), many national differences were forgotten for the time being. Jews served valiantly in the Red Army, organized partisan units behind German lines, and were treated as refugees in the interior of the Soviet Union, especially in the area of Central .... (46).

The toll of six million Jews, among them over one million Soviet and three million Polish Jews, is known in Hebrew as the .... (47), the Holocaust. The Nazi-led murders in the Soviet Union were carried out by special squads known as .... (48). It was the Red Army, however, which brought about the fall of Hitler in the East, with their final capture of the German capital city of .... (49) in 19.. (50). The pro-Jewish feeling lasted as late as 1948, when the Soviet government voted .... (for/against-51) the establishment of the State of Israel.

The advent of the cold war in 1948 brought an end to this period of good will. The dictator of the Soviet Union at that time, ... (52), pursued his internal anti-Jewish

APPENDIX

policies. Yiddish writers were purged and cultural life was strangled. A so-called .... (53) Plot was invented to undermine totally the status of Soviet Jews. The 1948-1953 period has been known infamously as the "..........." (54). Even with the dictator's death in 19.. (55), the Soviet anti-Zionist and anti-Jewish policies have continued.

Since the Russian Revolution over 50 years ago, no Hebrew Bibles, and only ....,000 (56) *Sidurim* have been published. Even the baking of *Matzot* has been hindered. Yiddish and Hebrew schools, theater, and press are virtually inoperative, even though some ....,000 (57) Jews indicated Yiddish as their mother tongue in the last Soviet census. The number of synagogues has dropped from over 1,000 in 1917 (in the Ukraine alone), to less than .... (58) today in all of the Soviet Union. There have been cases of economic trials and discrimination in jobs and political life.

Some Russians have expressed indignation, notably the poet .... (59) in his fiery poem .... (60). With the Six-Day War, the anti-Zionist tone of the Soviet propaganda has increased. So, too, have the protests of the Jews of the Soviet Union to leave to Israel and the West. International attention was given to a young Soviet Jewish engineer, named .... (61) and to 18 families from .... (62) who were either arrested, or detained from leaving the Soviet Union. More and more petitions have been reaching the West from trapped and desperate Soviet Jews. Almost inexplicably, the Soviet authorities have allowed ....,000 (63) Jews to emigrate from the Soviet Union since 1960. Many of those wishing to leave are subjected to harassment and intimidation. Many police raids were conducted in the wake of a hijacking attempt and the subsequent trial in December, 1970 in .... (64). The sentences imposed by the Soviet court brought worldwide protest, as did the imposition of an "education tax" in 1972.

The Jewish concept which expresses the intertwined fate of all Jews is termed .... (65). It asserts that these Soviet Jews are our people, and that they are a part of the past history and present concern of the American Jewish community, though separated by thousands of miles. As they nurtured us for over one hundred years, we must not allow them to die. We must affirm: "The Jewish people still lives!" .... (in Hebrew translation-66).

ANSWER SHEET

1. 14th-16th
2. Black
3. *Khazars*
4. England
5. France
6. "Germany"
7. *Va'ad Arbah Ha'aratzot*
8. Torah
9. Chmelnitsky
10. 1648-49
11. TaCH vTahT
12. 900,000
13. messiahs
14. Shabbtai Tzvi
15. *Chassidut*
16. BeSHT
17. *Mitnagdim*
18. Vilna
19. Poland
20. 72, 93, 95
21. Pale of Settlement
22. Napoleon
23. 1812
24. Nicholas I
25. emigration
26. 5
27. Zionism
28. Socialist
29. Trotsky
30. Ben-Gurion
31. Sharett
32. Eshkol
33. Meir
34. Kishinev
35. Beilis
36. February/March
37. October/November
38. *Yevsektsiya*
39. undermined
40. Yiddish
41. Birobidzhan
42. Soviet Union
43. Germany
44. Poland
45. June, 1941
46. Asia
47. *Shoah*
48. *Einsatzgruppen*
49. Berlin
50. 45
51. for
52. Stalin

APPENDIX

53. Doctor's
54. Black Years
55. 53
56. 10
57. 400
58. 60
59. Yevgeni Yevtushenko
60. Babi Yar
61. Boris Kochubievsky
62. Soviet Georgia
63. 65,000 (as of January, 1973)
64. Leningrad
65. *K'lal Yisrael*
66. *Ahm Yisrael Chai!*

BIBLIOGRAPHY

Adler, Cyrus (editor), *The Voice of America on Kishineff*. Jewish Publication Society, Philadelphia, 1904.

Aleichem, Shalom (pseud.), *The Old Country*. Crown Publishers, New York, 1946.

———, *Tevye's Daughters*, Crown Publishers, New York, 1949.

Altschuler, Mordechai (editor), *Jews of the Soviet Unionin the Years 1939-1953* (Hebrew). Academon, Jerusalem, 1971.

Aronson, Gregor and others (editors), *Russian Jewry 1917-1967*, trans. by Joel Carmichael. Thomas Yoseloff, New York, 1969.

Association of Latvian and Esthonian Jews in Israel, *The Jews in Latvia*. D. Ben-Nun Press, Tel Aviv, 1971.

Ausubul, Nathan (editor), *A Treasury of Jewish Folklore*. Crown Publisher, New York, 1948.

Babel, Isaac, *Collected Stories. Penguin Books*, London, 1961.

———, *The Lonely Years 1925-1939*. Edited by Natalie Babel: Farrar, Straus, and Company, New York, 1964.

———, *Lyubka the Cossack and Other Stories*. New American Library of World Literature, Inc., New York, 1963.

———, *You Must Know Everything*. Trans. by Max Howard: Farrar, Straus and Giroux, New York. 1966.

Baron, Salo, *The Russian Jew Under Tsars and Soviets*. Macmillan Co., New York, 1964.

Baum, Phil and Furst, Zev, *Briefing Kit for Travellers to the U.S.S.R.* American Jewish Congress, New York, 1972.

Billington, James H., *The Icon and the Axe: An Interpretive History of Russian Culture*. Alfred A. Knopf, Inc., New York, 1966.

Blackbook of Localities Whose Jewish Population Was Exterminated by the Nazis. Yad Vashem, Jerusalem, 1965.

Cang, Joel, *The Silent Millions.* Taplinger Publishing Co., Inc., New York, 1969.

Chamberlin, William Henry, *The Russian Revolution,* volume I. The Universal Library, New York, 1952.

Cherniavsky, Michael (editor), *Prologue to Revolution.* Prentice-Hall, New Jersey, 1967.

Chesnoff, Richard and others, *If Israel Lost the War.* Coward McCann, New York, 1969.

Cohen, Richard (editor), *Let My People Go.* Popular Library, New York, 1971.

Conference on Manifestations of Jewish Resistance, *Jewish Resistance During the Holocaust.* Alpha Press, Jerusalem, 1971.

Davidowicz, Lucy (editor), *The Golden Tradition.* Holt, Rinehart, and Winston, New York, 1967.

Dector, Moshe (editor), *Redemption! Jewish Freedom Letters from Russia.* American Conference on Soviet Jewry and Conference on the Status of Soviet Jews, New York, 1970.

Dubnow, S. M., *History of Jews in Russia and Poland.* Trans. by I. Friedlander, Jewish Publication Society, Philadelphia, volume I, 1916, volume II, 1918, volume III, 1920.

Dunlop, D. M., *The History of the Jewish Khazars.* Schocken Books, New York, 1967.

Efros, Israel (trans.), *Complete Poetic Works of Hayyim Nahman Bialik.* Volume I. Histadruth Ivrit of America, Inc., New York, 1948.

Eliav, Arie, *Between Hammer and Sickle.* New Amsterdam Library, New York, 1969.

Encyclopedia Judaica. Keter Publishing House, Ltd., Jerusalem, 1971.

Etinger, Shmuel, *Jewish History from the Days of Absolutism Until the Establishment of the State of Israel* (Hebrew). Academon, Jerusalem, 1968.

Florinsky, Michael (editor), *Encyclopedia of Russia and the Soviet Union.* McGraw-Hill Book Co., Inc., New York, 1961.

———, *The End of the Russian Empire.* Collier Books, New York, 1961.

———, *Russia: A History and Interpretation,* volumes I and II. Macmillan, 1963.

Frankel, Jonathan (editor), *Selected Problems in the History of Soviet Jewry* (Hebrew). Academon, Jerusalem, 1966.

Friedberg, Maurice, *The Jew in Post-Stalin Soviet Literature.* B'nai Brith International Council, Washington, D. C., 1970.

Gilbert, Martin, *Jewish History Atlas.* Weidenfeld and Nicolson, London, 1969.

Gilboa, Yehoshua, *The Black Years of Soviet Jewry.* Little, Brown and Company, Boston, 1971.

Gitelman, Zvi, *Jewish Nationality and Soviet Politics.* Princeton University Press, Princeton, N. J., 1972.

———, "The Jews," *Problems of Communism,* volume XVI, no. 5, Sept.-Oct., 1967.

Goldberg, Marie, *My Father, Shalom Aleichem.* Schocken Books, New York, 1968.

Goldman, Guido, *Zionism Under Soviet Rule.* Herzl Press, New York, 1960.

Ha'am ("The People"), November, 1916-May, 1918.

Halpern, Israel, *Eastern European Jewry, Historical Studies* (Hebrew). Magnes Press, Jerusalem, 1968.

Heschel, Abraham J., *The Earth is the Lord's.* Harper & Row, New York, 1968.

Howe, Irving (editor), *The Basic Writings of Trotsky.* Vintage Books, New York, 1963.

Jewish Chronicle Publications, *Jewish Travel Guide 1972.* London, 1972.

Jewry of the Soviet Union (Hebrew). Mifaley Tarbut Wechinuch Ltd., Tel Aviv, 1967.

BIBLIOGRAPHY

Kahane, Rabbi Meir, *Never Again!* Nash Publishing, Los Angeles, 1971.
Kochan, Lionel (editor), *The Jews in Soviet Russia Since 1917.* Oxford University Press, London, 1970.
Krausnick, Helmut, "The Persecution of the Jews," *Anatomy of the SS State.* Collins, London, 1968.
Lawrence, Gunther, *Three Million More.* Doubleday and Co., Inc., Garden City, New York, 1970.
Litvinoff, Barnett, *A Peculiar People.* Weidenfeld and Nicolson, London, 1969.
Lowenthal, Marvin (trans. and editor), *The Diaries of Theodore Herzl.* Grosset and Dunlop, New York, 1962.
Lunt, Horace G., *Fundamentals of Russian.* W. W. Norton and Co., New York, 1958.
Lvavi (Babitzky), Jacob, *The Jewish Colonization in Birobijan* (Hebrew). Historical Society of Israel, Jerusalem, 1965.
Ma'ariv, 1970-1972.
Maimonides, *Mishneh Torah.* Sefer Zeraim, standard editions.
Marcus, Jacob, *The Jew in the Medieval World, A Source Book 315-1791.* World Publishing Co., and Jewish Publicacation Society, Cleveland, New York, and Philadelphia, 1961.
Mendelsohn, Ezra, *Class Struggle in the Pale.* Cambridge University Press, Cambridge, Great Britain, 1970.
Morse, Arthur, *While Six Million Died.* Secker and Warburg, London, 1968.
New York Times, 1970-1972.
Patterson, David, *The Hebrew Novel in Czarist Russia.* Edinburgh University Press, Edinburgh, 1964.
Pollack, Allen, *The Soviet Union Vs. the Jewish People.* Council of Jewish Federations and Welfare Funds, New York, 1971.
Porath, Jonathan D., "The Editorial Policy of the Weekly *Ha'am.*" Master's Thesis, Columbia University, Graduate Faculties, 1968.

Postal, Bernard, and Abramson, Samuel, *The Traveller's Guide to the Jewish Landmarks of Europe*. Fleet Press Corporation, New York, 1971.

Pravda, 1953, 1970-1972.

Rosenberg, Louise, *Jews in the Soviet Union: An Annotated Bibliography 1967-1971*. American Jewish Committee, New York, 1971.

Rothenberg, Joshua, *The Jewish Religion in the Soviet Union*. Ktav, New York, 1971.

Rubin, Ronald (editor), *The Unredeemed: Anti-Semitism in the Soviet Union*. Quadrangle Books, Chicago, 1968.

Rusinek, Alla, *Like A Song, Like A Dream*. Charles Scribner's Sons, New York, 1973.

"Russia," *The Jewish Encyclopedia*. Funk and Wagnalls Company, volume X, pp. 518-575, New York, 1905.

Sachar, Howard, *The Course of Modern Jewish History*. Dell Publishing Co., New York, 1958.

Samuel, Maurice, *Blood Accusation: The Strange History of the Beilis Case*. Alfred A. Knopf, New York, 1966.

Schechtman, Joseph, *Zionism and Zionists in Soviet Russia*. Zionist Organization of America, New York, 1966.

Shmeruk, Kh. (editor), *Jewish Publications in the Soviet Union 1917-1960* (Hebrew). The Historical Society of Israel, Jerusalem, 1961.

Siddur Otzar Hatfillot, Vilna, 1914.

Singer, Isaac B., *The Slave*. Avon Books, New York, 1964.

Smolar, Boris, *Soviet Jewry Today and Tomorrow*. Macmillan Co., New York, 1971.

Suhl, Yuri (editor and trans.), *They Fought Back*. Paperback Library, Inc., New York, 1968.

Tsentsiper (Rafaeli), Aryeh, *In the Struggle for Redemption* (Hebrew), Tel Aviv, Dvir, 1957.

———, *The Pulsings of Redemption* (Hebrew). Tel Aviv, Dvir, 1952.

Weinreich, Uriel, *College Yiddish*. Yiddish Scientific Institute, New York, 1949.
Wiesel, Elie, *The Gates of the Forest*. Holt, Rinehart, and Winston, New York, 1966.
———, *The Jews of Silence*. Holt, Rinehart, and Winston, New York, 1966.
———, *Legends of Our Time*. Holt, Rinehart and Winston, New York, 1968.
———, *Souls on Fire*. Random House, New York, 1972.
Werth, Alexander. *Russia at War 1941-1945*. Pan Books Ltd., London, 1964.
West, Binjamin, *Struggles of a Generation*. Massadah Publishing Co., Tel Aviv, 1959.
Wilson, Edmund, *To the Finland Station*. W. H. Allen, London, 1940.
YIVO Annual of Jewish Social Studies, volume I. YIVO, New York, 1946.

Sources

A documentary history of this type relies entirely upon many different sources, and could not exist without them. I would like to express my thanks to the authors and publishers of the selections for their permission to reprint the material under their copyrights. They are listed by chapter to serve as a ready reference for those students who wish to do further reading in these books.

INTRODUCTORY UNIT

Letters From Moscow
Author's private correspondence.

Open Letter
American Jewish Conference on Soviet Jewry and Conference on the Status of Soviet Jews, *Redemption! Jewish Freedom Letters From Russia,* New York, pp. 28-29.

Letter From Soviet Georgia
Ibid., pp. 32-35.

A Soviet Reply on Jews: No. 1

© 1970 by The New York Times Company. Reprinted by permission. March 1, 5, 10, 1970.

A Soviet Reply on Jews: No. 2

Ibid., May 21, 1971.

TSARIST JEWRY UNIT

The Khazars

Jacob R. Marcus, *The Jew in the Medieval World, A Source Book: 315-1791,* Union of American Hebrew Congregations, New York, 1961, pp. 227-228.

Polish Jewry and the Va'ad Arbah Ha'aratzot

Israel Halpern, *Eastern European Jewish Historical Studies* (Hebrew), Magnes Press, Jerusalem, 1968, p. 80.

TaCH v'TahT and The Slave

Simon Dubnow, translated by I. Friedlander, *History of the Jews in Russia and Poland,* Vol. I, Jewish Publication Society, Philadelphia, 1916, pp. 145-146. (The Russian historian is not named by Dubnow).

The Slave and the Mitzvah of Pidyon Shevuyim

Moses Maimonides, *Mishneh Torah* (Hebrew), *Sefer Zeraim, Hilchot Matnot Ani'im,* 8:10. Author's translation.

The Kaddish of Levi Yitzchak
Taken from *A Treasury of Jewish Folklore*, edited by Nathan Ausubel. © 1948 by Crown Publishers, Inc. Used by permission of Crown Publishers, Inc., pp. 726-727.

The Fire
From *The Gates of the Forest* by Elie Wiesel. Translated by Frances Frenaye. Copyright © 1966 by Holt, Rinehart and Winston, Inc. Reprinted by permission of Holt, Rinehart and Winston, Inc. Introduction (unpaged).

A Russian Jewish View of Secular Authority
Samuel Pipe, "Napoleon in Jewish Folklore," *YIVO Annual of Jewish Social Studies*, Vol. I, YIVO Institute of Jewish Research, New York, 1946, pp. 299-300.

The Russian Jews and the Draft
Taken from *The Russian Jew Under Tsars and Soviets*, copyright © Salo W. Baron, Macmillan Company, New York, 1964, pp. 36-37, 37-38.

Into the Modern Age: The Haskalah
From "A Pilgrimage to Peretz Smolenskin" by Samual Leib Citron, translated by Lucy Dawidowicz, from *The Golden Tradition*, edited by Lucy S. Dawidowicz. Copyright © 1967 by Lucy S. Dawidowicz. Reprinted by permission of Holt, Rinehart and Winston, Inc., pp. 140-142.

Into the Modern Age: Zionism
From *The Diaries of Theodore Herzl*. Translated and edited by Marvin Lowenthal. Copyright © 1956 by The Dial Press, Inc. Used by permission of the publisher. pp. 403-405.

SOURCES

The Decline of Tsarist Jewry: The Kishinev Pogrom
Israel Efros, translator and editor, *Complete Poetic Works of Hayyim Nahman Bialik*, Vol. I., Histadruth Ivrit of America, Inc., New York, 1948, pp. 129-134.

The Decline of Tsarist Jewry: The Beilis Trial
Maurice Samuel, *Blood Accusation: The Strange History of the Beiliss Case.* Copyright © 1966 by Maurice Samuel. Used by permission of Alfred Knopf, Inc. P. 213.

A Prayer for the Tsar
Siddur Otzar Hatfilot, Vilna, 1914, p. 359. Author's translation.

The Jewish Population Explosion
The Russian Jew Under Tsars and Soviets, *op cit.*, p. 77. (See Baron's footnote #2, page 363, concerning problems relating to the reliability of these figures).

SOVIET JEWRY UNIT
THE REVOLUTION UNTIL THE SHOAH

"Vilna in Distress"
"Ha'am," May 12, 1917. Cited in "The Editorial Policy of the Weekly Ha'am," Jonathan D. Porath, Master's Thesis Columbia University Graduate Faculties, 1968, p. 38.

"The Election Campaign"
"Ha'am," January 15, 1918. Author's translation.

"The Separation of Church and State"
W. H. Chamberlin, *The Russian Revolution: 1917-1921*, Vol. I. Copyright © 1935 by The Macmillan Company. Renewed 1963 by William Henry Chamberlin. pp. 497-498.

Jews in the Communist Party
Listing assembled with the aid of Professor Leon Shapiro and the *Encyclopedia Judaica*, Keter Publishing House Ltd., Jerusalem, 1971.

Leon Trotsky and the Jews
Irving Howe, editor, *The Basic Writings of Trotsky*. Copyright © 1963 by Random House, Inc. Used by permission of Random House, Inc. pp. 207-208, 214.

The Yevsekstiya
The Russian Jews Under Tsars and Soviets, op cit., p. 208.

Isaac Babel
Reprinted by permission of S. G. Phillips, Inc., from *The Collected Stories* by Isaac Babel. Copyright © 1955 by S. G. Phillips, Inc. pp. 166-168.

The Soviet Jewish Economy
Shmuel Etinger, *Jewish History from the Days of Absolutism Until the Establishment of the State of Israel* (Hebrew), Academon, Jerusalem, 1968, p. 284.

Soviet Jewish Book Publishing

Kh. Shmeruk, editor, *Jewish Publications in the Soviet Union 1917-1960* (Hebrew), the Historical Society of Israel, Jerusalem, 1961, pp. 64-69, 113 (Hebrew listing).

Publishing in the Hebrew Language

Ibid., pp. 17-41, 406-409.

The Pre-Shoah Soviet Jew

Benjamin West, *Struggle of a Generation*, Massada Publishing Company, Ltd., Tel Aviv, 1959, pp. 71-72.

SOVIET JEWRY UNIT
THE SHOAH

Einsatzgruppen

From the book *Anatomy of the SS State* by Helmut Krausnick, published by Walker and Company, Inc., New York, New York. © 1968 by William Collins Sons, pp. 60-63.

Russia At War

From the book *Russia At War: 1941-1945*, by Alexander Werth. Copyright © 1964 by Alexander Werth. Published by E. P. Dutton and Company, Inc., and used with their permission. Pp. 793-794, 796, 671.

The Jewish Anti-Fascist Committee

Struggles of a Generation, op cit., p. 22.

Jewish Resistance: The Partisans
Taken from *They Fought Back*, edited and translated by Yuri Suhl. © 1967 by Yuri Suhl. Used by permission of Crown Publishers, Inc. pp. 290-291.

The Blackbook
Yad Vashem, *Blackbook of the Localities Whose Jewish Population Was Exterminated by the Nazis. Jerusalem*, 1965, pp. x-xi, and Professor Leon Shapiro.

The Mitzvah of Remembering
Moses Maimonides, *Sefer Hamitzvot* (Hebrew), #189. Author's translation.

SOVIET JEWRY UNIT
THE BLACK YEARS AND CONTEMPORARY SOVIET JEWRY

The Black Years: Golda Meir in Moscow
Struggles of a Generation, op cit., p. 44

The Black Years: The "Doctors' Plot"
Yehoshua A. Gilboa, *The Black Years of Soviet Jewry 1939-1935*. Little, Brown and Company, Boston, 1971, pp. 295-296, 301. Quoted are selections from *Pravda* (January 13, 1953) and *Trud* (January 17, 1953).

Post-War Soviet Yiddish Publishing

Jewish Publications in the Soviet Union 1917-1960, op. cit., pp. 64-69 (Hebrew listing) and Professor Leon Shapiro.

The Use of Yiddish in the Soviet Union

Mordechai Altschuler, "Trends in the Demographic Character of the Jewish Settlement in the Soviet Union," in *Jewry in the Soviet Union* (Hebrew), Mifaley Tarbut Wechinuch Ltd., Tel Aviv, 1967, p. 9.

Soviet Jewry in the 1960's: "Babi Yar"

Marie Syrkin, translator, *Hadassah Magazine*, New York, 1971. Reprinted by permission.

Soviet Jewry in the 1970's: Jewish Activists Challenge the Soviet Government

Exodus, No. 4, 1971, reprinted and translated by *Soviet Jewish Affairs*, London, pp. 33-34.

The Education Tax

United Synagogue Commission on Social Action, *Judaism and Social Action*, New York, November, 1972, p. 2 (among others).

Russian Jewish Emigration

Harry Trimborn, "Jewish Emigration May Pave Way for Better Soviet-Israeli Relations," copyright, 1972, *Los Angeles Times*. Reprinted by permission, January 6, 1972.

NOTES

NOTES

NOTES

NOTES

NOTES

4 FT.

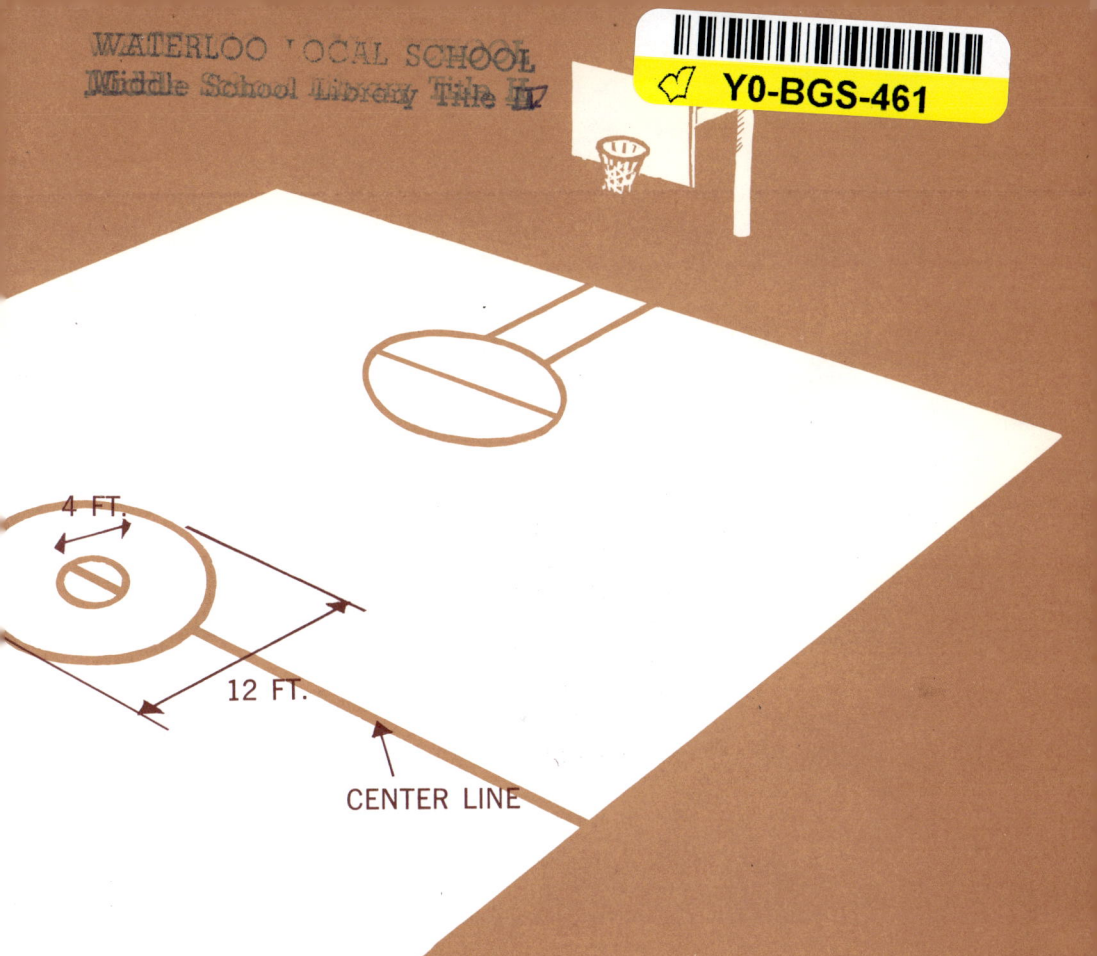

12 FT.

CENTER LINE

High school basketball courts are 84 ft. by 50 ft.; college and pro courts are 94 ft. by 50 ft.

BASKETBALL SUPERSTARS
THREE GREAT PROS
BY LES ETTER

GARRARD PUBLISHING COMPANY
CHAMPAIGN, ILLINOIS

Sports Consultant:
COLONEL RED REEDER
Former Member of the West Point Coaching Staff and Special Assistant to the West Point Director of Athletics

Library of Congress Cataloging in Publication Data

Etter, Les.
    Basketball superstars: three great pros.

  (Sports library)
    SUMMARY: Brief biographies stressing the careers of basketball stars Wilt Chamberlain, Jerry West, and Oscar Robertson.
    1. Chamberlain, Wilton Norman, 1936–   —Juvenile literature. 2. West, Jerry, 1938–   —Juvenile literature. 3. Robertson, Oscar, 1938–   —Juvenile literature. [1. Chamberlain, Wilton Norman, 1936– 2. West, Jerry, 1938–   3. Robertson, Oscar, 1938–   4. Basketball—Biography] I. Title.
GV884.A1E87   796.32′3′0922   [920]   73-9659
ISBN 0-8116-6667-0

Photo credits:

United Press International: pp. 1, 3, 4, 6, 8, 21, 22, 26, 31, 32, 37, 40, 45, 55, 62 (both), 68, 70, 77, 88, 92, 95 (both), jacket
University of Cincinnati (William Whitteker): p. 80
Wide World Photos: pp. 11, 18, 42, 52, 85

Copyright © 1974 by Les Etter
All rights reserved. Manufactured in the U.S.A.

CONTENTS

A Game for Giants 5

Wilt Chamberlain
    Record Maker 9

Jerry West
    Clutch Player 43

Oscar Robertson
    All-Around Player 71

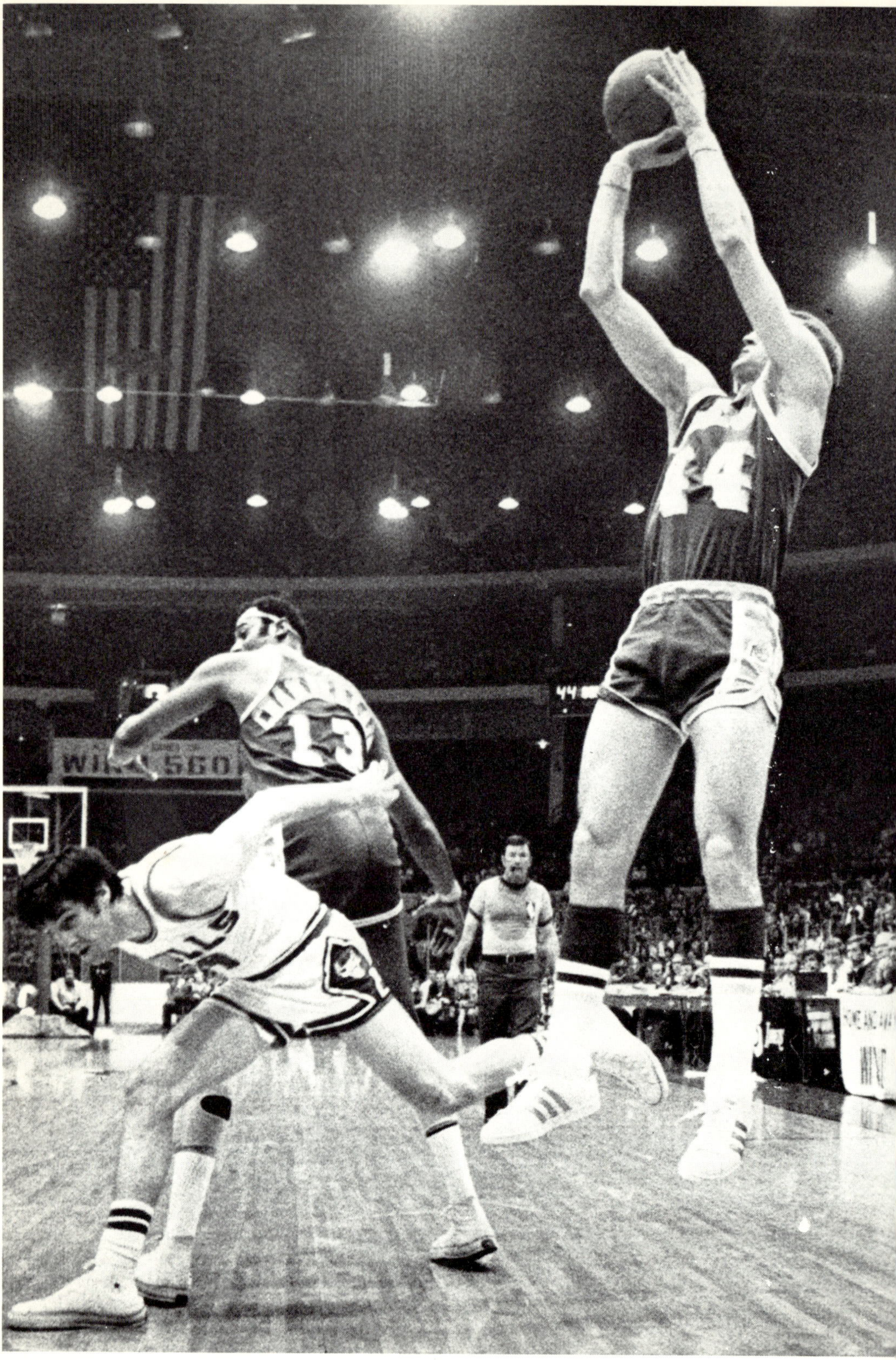

A Game for Giants

Two giants crouch in the center circle of the basketball court. The referee holds the ball for the toss-up. The fans sit on the edges of their seats. They know this will be a fast, hard-fought game, for these men are pros. They are some of the best players in the world.

Suddenly the referee's whistle sounds. The ball shoots up from his hand. Both centers leap high. The game is on!

Passing, faking, pivoting, the tall players move the ball up the court. One man steals the ball and steps back. There's a quick jump shot and a basket. Before the

Laker Jerry West drives past Walt Frazier of the Knicks on his way to the basket.

fans can cheer, the players have moved the ball to the other end of the court. Until the buzzer sounds the fast play won't let up. It will be action all the way.

Thousands of fans crowd into big arenas each season to watch pro games. Millions more watch on TV. Pro basketball is one of America's most popular and exciting sports.

Most professional players were once college stars. They are all fine players who must become even better to hold their own in rugged pro games. The players are paid to win. They must work every minute of every game to do just that. The schedule —82 games before play-offs—is tiring. The play is hard and sometimes rough. Injuries are common. Pro players need more than talent; they must also have great courage and determination.

This book is about three heroes of pro basketball who have become all-time great players—Wilt Chamberlain, Jerry West, and Oscar Robertson.

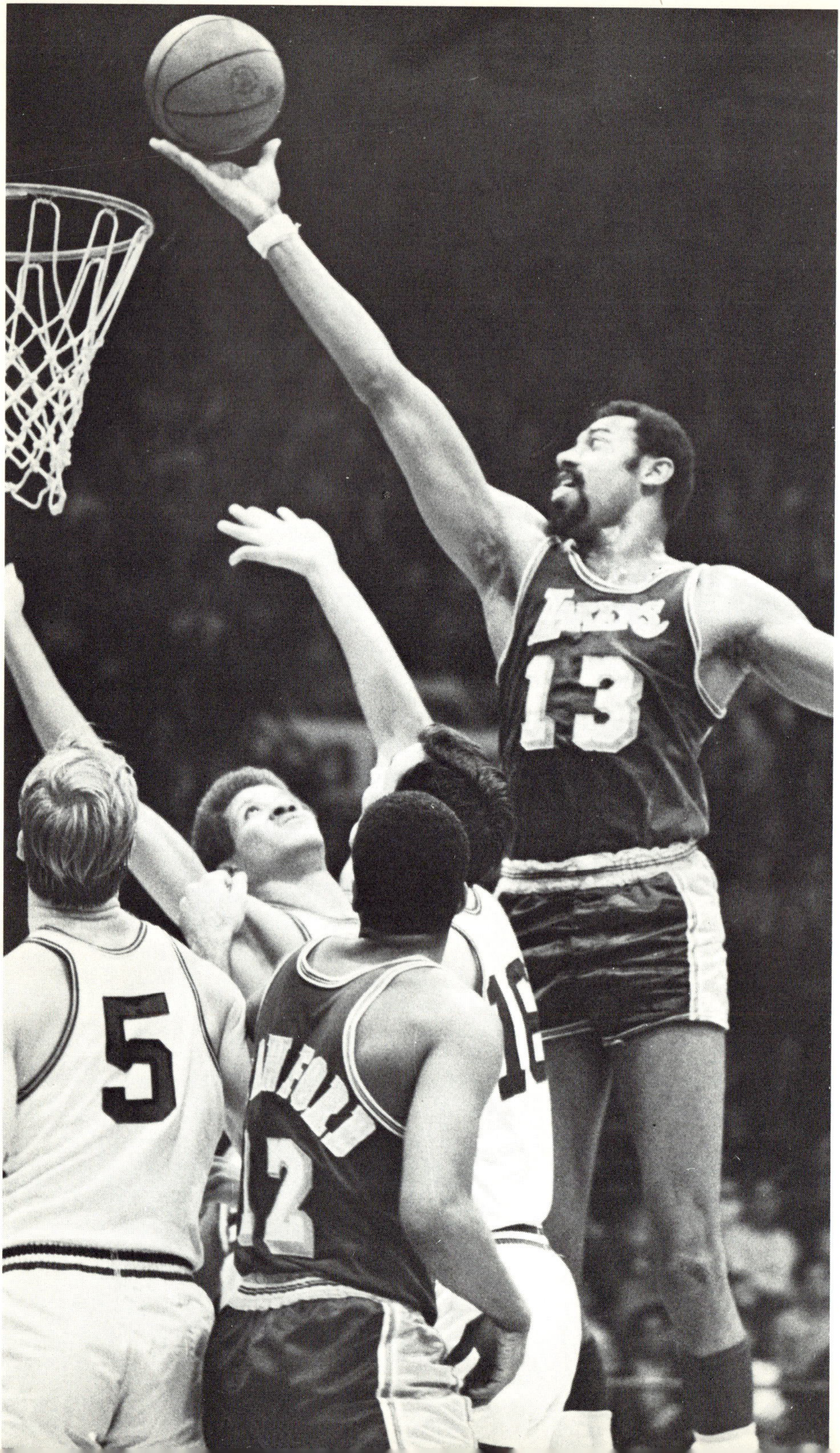
LAKERS
13
5

Wilt Chamberlain
Record Maker

The Philadelphia Warriors were leading the New York Knicks by a wide margin. Less than 50 seconds were left to play in the game. Yet the fans were on their feet, cheering wildly.

"Give it to Wilt!" they shouted. "Give Wilt the ball!"

Wilt Chamberlain, the giant Warrior center, bounded high above three defenders. He took a pass and reached above the basket. The ball shot down through the rim like a bullet.

One hundred points by Wilt Chamberlain!

Excited fans dashed out onto the court. There were still 46 seconds left, and officials tried to clear the floor. But no one paid any attention to them. Everyone crowded around Wilt to slap him on the back or grasp his hand. Finally officials moved the fans off the court, and the players finished the game. The Philadelphia Warriors won, 169–147.

As the buzzer was sounded, Wilt Chamberlain's face broke into a smile, and he waved to the cheering crowd. Wilt had done the impossible that March night in 1962. He had become the very first player in the history of the National Basketball Association (NBA) to score 100 points in a single game.

"I didn't do it alone," Wilt told reporters gathered around him. "If the other fellows hadn't kept feeding the ball to me, it couldn't have happened."

Wilt Chamberlain sinks another basket, bringing his score to a record-breaking 100 points in a single game.

While the 100-point score made newspaper headlines, Wilt set other records that night. He shot 36 baskets in 63 tries, made 28 of 32 free throws, and he scored 31 points in one quarter and 59 for a half.

Of all the records he set that night, the free-throw mark must have meant the most to Wilt. For free-throw shooting was one of his few weaknesses. He had spent many hours practicing at the foul line to improve his skill. Wilt had always worked to make his play perfect, and now in one record-setting game, he had come close.

Wilton Norman Chamberlain was born August 21, 1936, in the Haddington district of West Philadelphia, where most of the people are black. He lived with his parents and eight brothers and sisters in a big, lively household. The Chamberlains were a happy, church-going family. Though there was no money for extras, Wilt's father made enough to support them comfortably. Wilt had lots of friends in the neighborhood. In school he was a good student, well liked by his teachers.

While he was still in elementary school, Wilt saw his first basketball game, but he wasn't impressed. It seemed to him to be a "sissy" sport. He thought the games played on the street with his friends were better. He especially liked "wall ball," in which a rubber ball is bounced against the side of a house and batted back by the players.

Wilt was good at such games even though he was unusually tall and thin. By the age of ten, he was so tall he often bumped his head against low doorways. Once while playing in an empty house, he ran into a pipe near the ceiling. The other boys teased him in a friendly way, and told him to "dip under" such low objects. That's how he got his first nickname, "The Dipper."

As the years passed Wilt kept outgrowing his clothes faster than his parents could buy new ones. One summer he grew four inches, and his father had to raise all the light fixtures in the house.

As Wilt grew taller and taller, he noticed that people on the street stared at him. He heard their laughter and unkind remarks. He began to change. He kept to himself so much that his friends called him a loner and his parents worried about him.

Then one day, soon after he entered Shoemaker Junior High School, Wilt went to the gym to watch basketball practice. Suddenly the coach blew his whistle. "You, son," he called to Wilt. "Why aren't you out for basketball? We can use a tall boy like you."

Wilt was too surprised to answer. He saw that the other boys had stopped playing and were watching him. "Look at the long arms on that kid," one boy shouted. Another yelled, "Hey, big boy! Can I be on your team?"

Right then a whole new world opened up for young Wilt Chamberlain. He found friends who admired his height. They talked about how well he handled the ball. It all seemed to come so easily that he surprised himself. Wilt played every chance he got.

His interest naturally took Wilt to Haddington Center, the local recreation building. Basketball was the big sport at Haddington. Play there was fast and rough. Wilt found that basketball wasn't a sissy game after all. Elbows and even fists were freely used. Most of the players were older and stronger than Wilt, and he took a beating at first. But before long he learned to fight back.

James "Blinky" Brown, an instructor at the Center, later spoke of Wilt's early days there.

"If you cracked Wilt with an elbow," chuckled Brown, "he didn't hit back. But the next time you shot, he'd block it or steal the ball from you. He was already learning to use his height and quickness."

Wilt never forgot Haddington Center. He formed many lifelong friendships there. And in 1960, several years after Wilt left the Center, his friends set up a Wilt Chamberlain Award. Each year the honor goes to the boy who shows outstanding "leadership, service, and participation." Wilt has often returned to present the award.

Wilt Chamberlain was just sixteen when he entered Overbrook High School in West

Philadelphia. By this time he stood 6 feet, 11 inches tall and weighed 200 pounds. He wore a size 17 collar and size 13 shoes. His long thin arms and legs made him look even taller. The Overbrook basketball coach, of course, quickly put him on the team.

A reporter, watching his early games, called him "Wilt the Stilt." The nickname stuck, but Wilt hated it. "It makes me sound like some sort of ugly bird," he said. He liked being called "The Dipper" much better.

During the three years Wilt played basketball at Overbrook, the team lost only three games. Wilt scored an average of 37 points for each game. Twice he scored 90 points. The other teams often placed two and sometimes three men to guard him. But he was seldom stopped.

By the time Wilt was a junior at

Overbrook, he was famous. Stories about the young Philadelphia high school star were being printed in newspapers and magazines everywhere. Many college coaches wanted him to play on their teams. Even before he graduated, more than 200 colleges offered him scholarships.

Letters and phone calls came to the Chamberlain home. College coaches and

At eighteen, Wilt (left) was already famous. He is seen here with his admiring family.

scouts made special trips to talk to Wilt and his parents. The NBA professional teams wanted him to play. The Harlem Globetrotters, an all-black team that put on exhibition games all over the world, asked him to join them.

Wilt already had made up his mind. "I want a college education first," he told his folks. "Then I'd like to try the pro game if I play well in college." Mr. and Mrs. Chamberlain agreed with their son.

Wilt politely turned down the pro offers. Then he visited colleges all around the country. Finally he decided to go to the University of Kansas because it was a good school and it had a strong basketball team. He liked "Phog" Allen, who had coached the Kansas Jayhawks to many championships.

At that time freshmen couldn't play on the varsity. But the fans wanted to see

Wilt play anyway. Fourteen thousand of them came to his first freshman game against the Jayhawk varsity. Many of them drove long distances to see the young basketball star. Wilt didn't disappoint the Jayhawk fans.

When he trotted out on the floor for the warm-up drill, Wilt towered above his teammates. The huge crowd talked excitedly about his size.

"Seven feet tall," gasped one fan. "Looks more like ten feet to me. He's going to be a winner all right!"

Another man disagreed. "Yeah?" he scoffed. "We haven't seen him play yet. The varsity will run away from a big guy like that."

No one ran away from Wilt Chamberlain that night. The varsity couldn't even catch him. He scored 42 points to lead the freshmen in an upset victory.

Young Wilt, in frosh uniform, seemed to be everywhere in the freshman-varsity game.

Wilt's first varsity game the next season was even more exciting. Kansas faced the Northwestern Wildcats, one of the country's strongest teams.

At the start Wilt tapped the ball away from the Northwestern center. Racing downcourt he took a pass under the Wildcat basket. His right hand shot up,

21

Wilt leaps into the air to grab a rebound from a California player in a 1956 game.

and the ball dropped through the hoop. Two points!

Wilt scored 11 points before the Wildcats got a basket. Even with two men guarding him, he scored 52 points and got 31 rebounds that night. Both were new records. Kansas won, 87–69.

Wilt soon became the highest college scorer in the country. He made baskets as easily against college teams as he had against Philadelphia high school teams.

A reporter asked a rival coach what sort of defense could stop Wilt. "Patience," replied the coach. "Someday he'll graduate."

Wilt made All-American two years in a row, and Kansas lost few games. By his junior season the Jayhawks had worked out a style of play that seldom changed. Wilt would hurry to his pivot position and stand there, his hands held high, waiting for the ball.

Defensive players, trying to block his shots, would crowd around him so that he could hardly move. Play often became rough under the basket. Wilt didn't have a chance to play real basketball.

Suddenly Wilt decided he'd had enough, and he left Kansas at the end of his junior year. He wanted to turn pro as soon as possible. But under NBA rules the Dipper could not play with an NBA team until his college class had graduated. He would have to wait one more year. While waiting, he joined the Harlem Globetrotters on a world tour. It was a good year for Wilt. The visits in many countries led him to a lifelong interest in learning foreign languages. The large salary gave him a chance to save money.

The first thing Wilt did when he got back was to buy a new home for his parents. His basketball future seemed fairly well decided. At that time pro teams had first claim on high school stars in their geographical area, and Wilt, of course, was the home town draft choice of the Philadelphia Warriors. Now that his college class had graduated, Wilt was free to accept the draft and play for the Warriors.

"Wilt the Stilt," as most fans called him, was not measured when he joined the Warriors in 1959. He gave his height as 7 feet, 1/16 inch tall and his weight as 275 pounds. Later he added an inch to his height to make it 7 feet, 1 1/16 inches tall.

Wilt, now 23 years old, was eager to match himself against the NBA's best players. His first real test came when the Warriors met the Celtics at the Boston Garden. Both teams were undefeated in preseason games. The Celtics' star, Bill Russell, was famous for his shot blocking and rebounding. Wilt's scoring ability was

With rebound in hand, Wilt tries to escape from the heavy guarding of Celtic Bill Russell.

already well known. Everyone wanted to see if Chamberlain's scoring punch could beat Russell's defensive play.

Bill planned to surprise his rookie rival. He had a deadly jump shot of his own near the basket. As the game opened, he faked a pass and jumped high. Wilt leaped even higher to smack the ball away. Russell tried again, and Wilt blocked again. After a few more tries, Bill told a teammate, "I'm retiring my jumper against this guy—he's too good."

Wilt outscored his opponent, but Russell led in rebounds and was perfect from the free-throw line. Wilt missed 6 of 12 foul shots, and Boston won, 115–106. It was the first of many exciting battles between these two great players.

At the end of the season Wilt had grabbed more rebounds than Russell and led the league in scoring. But in the Eastern Play-Off, Boston defeated Philadelphia. So Russell was the winner, and Chamberlain was the loser. After that, whenever these two teams met, the game ended in the same way. Wilt would lead in scoring, but the Boston team would win. Wilt was determined to beat the Celtics.

During that first season Wilt was chosen "Rookie of the Year" and "Most Valuable

Player" in the NBA. Many experts thought he was the best rookie ever. Others said all he had was size.

Most people agreed that Wilt was one of the cleanest players in the league. He never liked rough play. Once he and Johnny Green of the Knicks leaped toward the basket together. Wilt could have dunked the ball, but he let his shot be blocked. "He knew he'd have broken my hand if he'd dunked," Green said later.

As Wilt's scoring average rose, other teams tried harder than ever to stop him. When he complained about the rough play under the basket, a newsman asked him why he didn't fight back.

"If I punch someone, what does that prove?" Wilt replied. "That's not basketball."

Instead of fighting, Wilt just went ahead and played great ball. Against Boston and

Bill Russell in his second season, Wilt got 55 rebounds for a new single-game record. He led all scorers and rebounders again, but Boston won the NBA championship.

Russell always tried to play his best against Chamberlain. He worked out new ways to block Wilt's shots or steal rebounds from him. But he didn't always succeed. One night the Dipper scored 49 points against him. When Chamberlain was at *his* best he could not be stopped. Usually when the season ended, Wilt owned more new records, but it was Bill and the Celtics who had the title.

In 1961–62 Wilt was high scorer once more as the Warriors moved into the Eastern Division Play-Off. Still that season, too, Boston beat them and went on to become the national champion.

Philadelphia fans grew restless. They were tired of seeing Boston finish in first place. If Chamberlain could score 50 points a game, why couldn't the Warriors win the title? they wondered.

The fans blamed Wilt. "All Chamberlain thinks of is his scoring average," they said. "He's not a team player." Many people stopped going to games, and the Warriors were moved to San Francisco. When a new coach named Alex Hannum was hired, he urged Wilt to shoot less and pass more. Wilt agreed. His scoring dropped, but his passing helped San Francisco to win the Western Division Play-Off the next season.

Once again, Boston was waiting for him in the NBA championship finals. The move to the West hadn't changed Wilt's luck. Wilt played well—but Boston won the title.

In January 1965, the Warriors traded Chamberlain to the 76ers, a new club in Philadelphia. This move put him in the

Back in Philadelphia with the 76ers, Wilt, wearing a nose guard, goes up for a rebound against Reggie Harding of Detroit.

Alex Hannum, new coach of the 76ers, watches a tense moment of play.

same division with Russell and the Celtics once more.

With Wilt in the lineup, the 76ers finished third in the regular season and won a place in the play-offs against Boston. In the play-offs Wilt was at his best. The 76ers fought Boston right down to the final moments of the seventh game.

With five seconds left, Boston led by a single point, 110–109. Russell tried to pass inbounds above Wilt's waving arms. But the ball struck the backboard and bounced outside—Philadelphia's ball. Then Hal Greer passed to Chet Walker for the 76ers' final shot, but Boston's John Havlicek stole the ball, and the Celtics won again. Wilt had scored 30 points and grabbed 26 rebounds, but as always, the Celtics had the title.

In 1966 the Celtics beat the 76ers again in the play-offs. Then things began to happen. Alex Hannum left the Warriors to coach the 76ers. He brought in younger players and built the team around Wilt. He placed the giant center beneath the basket to hold the ball, ready to pass to his mates. Wilt took few shots himself, but set up little Hal Greer and other teammates for jump shots or lay-ups. His unselfish play helped give the 76ers a 68–13 season record, the best in NBA history. His scoring average was his lowest, but he was the Most Valuable Player once more.

The 76ers whizzed into the Eastern Division finals to meet Boston. Philadelphia fans dared to hope—until they remembered Boston had been the champs nine of the past ten seasons. Could Wilt and his mates break the Celtics' hold on the title this time?

The crowd was in an uproar as Wilt and Bill Russell crouched for the opening tip-off. With an amazing leap, the Dipper slapped the ball away from his rival and into Hal Greer's hands.

Wilt began batting away shots and stealing rebounds right from the start. He outmatched Russell, now Boston's player-coach, at his own game. Midway in the third quarter the 76ers led, 91–66.

Then Russell started a Boston rally. The Philadelphia fans grew silent as the score became closer. Was their title dream about to be spoiled again?

Suddenly Wilt's huge hand reached up to grab the ball near the foul circle. He threw it like a baseball to the far end of the court. Hal Greer took it in to score an easy lay-up. The play broke the Boston rally, and the 76ers went on to win, 127–113.

Chamberlain continued to play some of his best basketball as Philadelphia won the next two games. In the second one the Celtics took an early lead, but Wilt outfought Russell for rebounds and set up the winning plays. The Dipper grabbed 41 rebounds in the third game, and now the 76ers were only a game away from the division title. Then came the fourth game, and Russell hit his stride. He outplayed Wilt, and the Celtics won 121–117.

Boston started fast in the fifth game, and they still led in the third period. Then Wilt's steady passing to Wally Jones, the

76ers guard, brought eight baskets, and Philadelphia went ahead, 100–95.

Even Bill Russell couldn't stop Wilt. After the Dipper stuffed a rebound through the hoop in the last quarter, the 76ers went on a scoring spree to win, 140–116.

Wilt had finally taken the title from the Celtics. But he did not join in the Philadelphia cheering. Instead he said quietly, "Let's wait. The big one's still ahead." He meant the championship play-off with the San Francisco Warriors, the Western Division winner.

In the first play-off game, the 76ers took a 19-point lead. But at the end, with six seconds left to play, they found themselves tied with the Warriors. Nate Thurmond, the San Francisco center, leaped high to take the last shot, but Wilt blocked it, and the game went into overtime before the 76ers won, 141–135.

Chamberlain battles with his old rival, Bill Russell, for control of the ball during the 1967 Play-Offs with the Celtics.

In the sixth game the Warriors trailed by one point with fifteen seconds left. Warrior Rick Barry tried to shoot the winning basket. But Wilt's arm shot out to knock the ball away. The 76ers had won the final game and Philadelphia fans had their National Champion at last!

Wilt walked proudly off the court. After eight years his team had finally made it.

In 1968 he was traded to the Los Angeles Lakers, where he joined Elgin Baylor and Jerry West. The next season these three sparked the Lakers to the Western Division crown. Then they met Boston for the NBA title. Once more Wilt and Bill Russell fought for every rebound. Late in the seventh game, the Dipper hurt his knee. From the bench he sadly watched Boston win by two points to become the NBA champ again.

In 1972 Wilt and Jerry West led Los

Angeles on a 33-game winning streak, the longest in the history of any pro sport. The Lakers won the Western Division to face the New York Knicks for another chance at the national title.

The Knicks won the first game. Then the Lakers won three in a row with Wilt playing at his best. He blocked shots and snatched rebounds off the backboard, and he scored well.

But the Dipper had hurt his right wrist, and he entered the fifth game with his hand heavily taped. The fans saw the bandages and wondered how long he'd last. They soon found out. The giant center played his finest game of the season to lead the Lakers to a 114–100 win. Los Angeles had its first NBA championship, and Wilt was the Most Valuable Player. The fans cheered him wildly when he left the floor.

Wilt knocks the wind out of Jerry Lucas of the Knicks in a 1972 championship game.

For Wilt's fans, the victory had a very special meaning. Everyone knew he was the best scorer in NBA history, and that he had beaten Bill Russell's rebounding record early in the season. Now they saw that he had willingly changed his style of play for the good of the team. In 1973 this change in style again helped carry the Lakers to the division championship. In the hard-fought NBA Play-Off Wilt played a team game to the end. The title went to the Knicks, but now even his old critics had to agree that Wilt was more than just a great player—he was a great team man, too.

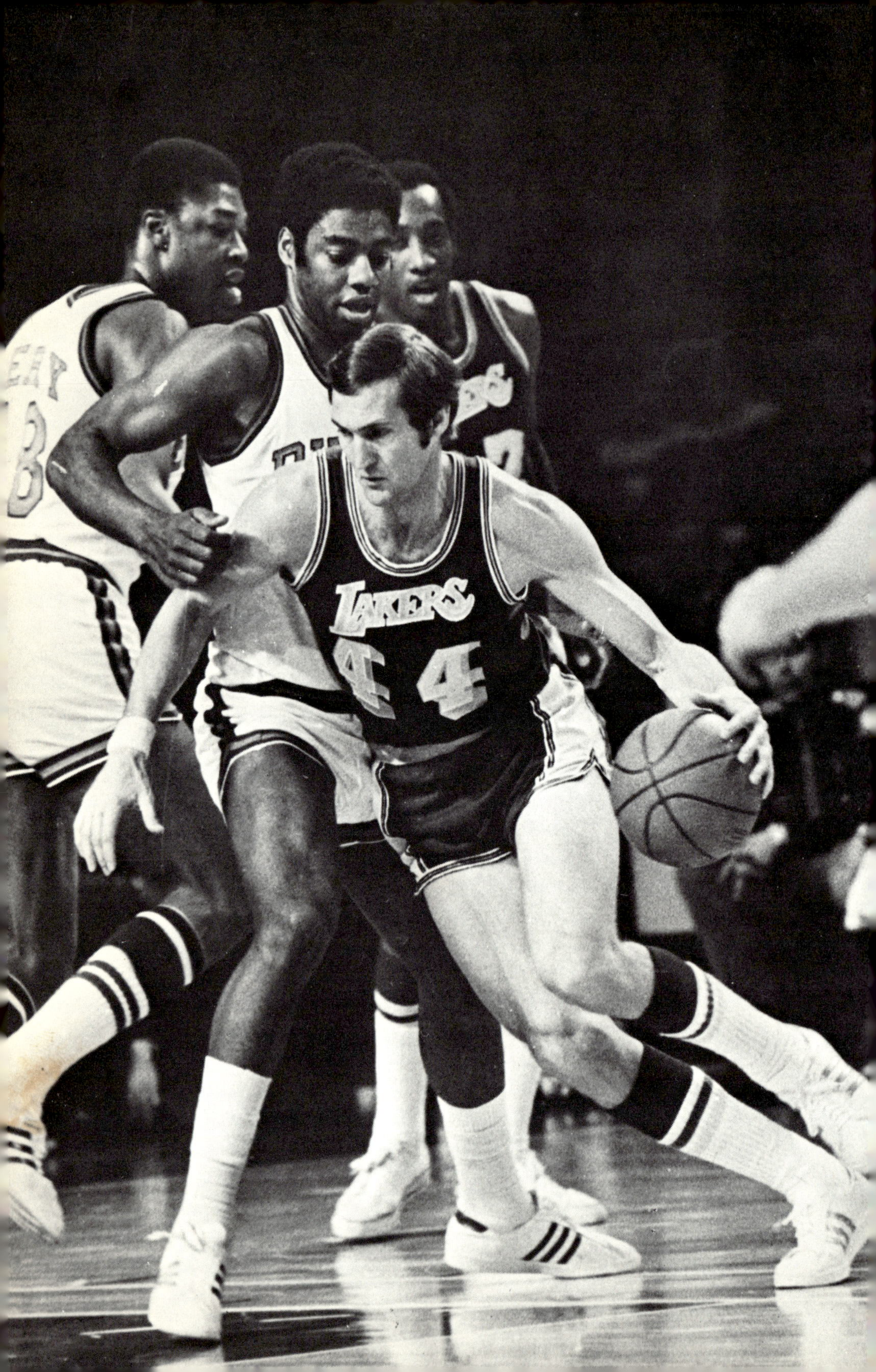
LAKERS
44

Jerry West
Clutch Player

A sportswriter once called him "Mr. Clutch" because of his skill at winning close games. That nickname described Jerry West perfectly.

There are no figures to prove how many times Jerry has won for the Los Angeles Lakers in the final seconds of an exciting game. But when the score was tied, or the Lakers were a few points behind, Jerry West usually found some way to win. It was not always his last basket that won a game. Sometimes a quick pass to a teammate set up the winning play. Other times he grabbed a rebound or stole the ball.

In the third game of the 1970 NBA championship, Jerry was in just such a tight spot. The Lakers were playing the New York Knicks in a best-of-seven series. The first team to win four games would become the NBA champion. Each team had won one game so far.

Sparked by West, their backcourt ace, the Lakers led at halftime, 56–42. Then Jerry jammed his left thumb. It was a painful injury, but he refused to leave the floor. He just gritted his teeth and played harder than ever, shooting with his right hand.

During the third period the Knicks began to catch up. In the fourth quarter they tied the score at 100 points apiece. The final seconds ticked away swiftly.

Jerry West goes high into the air in the 1970 NBA Championship Finals. His shot is blocked by a determined Knicks player.

Suddenly Dave DeBusschere of the Knicks caught a pass twenty feet from the basket. He whirled and fired the ball through the hoop with one quick motion. New York led, 102–100. Only three seconds remained as the Lakers took the ball.

Jerry West grabbed the in-bounds pass from Wilt Chamberlain and dribbled the ball up the floor. A glance at the clock showed him that he had one second to play. The Lakers' basket was an impossible 55 feet away.

Gathering every bit of his wiry strength, Jerry leaped high. A jump shot flew off his right hand.

"No—no!" screamed DeBusschere.

The ball rolled around the rim, then dropped through the net just as the buzzer ended the regulation game at 102–102. For an instant the crowd was stunned. Then a mighty shout went up.

But this time Jerry's thrilling play was not enough to win the game. The Knicks came back from the shock of that basket to win in overtime, 111–108.

When a reporter asked about his "desperation shot," Jerry frowned. "I wouldn't call it that. I just aimed it and got my body behind it. I've made shots that long in practice—but never with so much at stake."

All the coaches and players who know Jerry think he's one of basketball's best. One coach had this to say about him: "West is not big for a pro—not at 6 feet, 3 inches tall and 185 pounds—but he's got everything. He can shoot, he has quick hands, and he's fast as lightning. Add courage and dedication to the game, and you've got Jerry West."

Dedication to the game—that has always been one of Jerry's strongest points. From the first day he held a ball in his hands, his love for the game never left him.

Jerry West was born in Cheylan, West Virginia, May 28, 1938. The family lived in a two-story house on the edge of the tiny village.

Jerry's first basketball teacher was his older brother, David, who was later killed in the Korean War. Together they played with other boys in a neighbor's backyard. A hoop nailed to a homemade backboard was a basket. The court was the hard-packed ground. Jerry liked the game so much that he spent all the time he could shooting baskets.

When he first went out for basketball at East Bank High, near Cheylan, Jerry had a lot to learn. Even as a sophomore the next season, he did not exactly get off to a flying start. He first played in the fourth game of the season, on New Year's Day,

1954, and didn't even score. Still, he did make 12 points in another game when the coach had to use him because several regulars were ill.

Jerry's brief scoring splurge didn't help much. A few weeks later he broke his ankle while trying to block a shot. He spent the rest of the season with his foot in a cast. But East Bank's team wound up with a 16–4 record—good enough to take them to the second round of the regional meet.

As soon as Jerry's foot healed he began to practice harder than ever. By the end of the next season he was the star of the varsity team. Then, as a senior, he led his team to the state championship and scored 39 points in the final game. In his honor East Bank High School changed its name to *West* Bank for one week.

Colleges in many parts of the country

wanted Jerry to play for them. He was offered so many athletic scholarships that he became confused. Finally he asked his mother what to do.

"I know what I'd do," she said. "I'd go to the college in the state where they know me best."

That was exactly what Jerry wanted to hear. He had always dreamed of playing for a college in his home state. Besides, he liked Fred Schaus, the West Virginia University coach, who had often watched his high school games.

The change from a small high school to a large college full of strangers wasn't easy for Jerry West. His classroom work dropped, and that was discouraging. But on the basketball court it was a different story. He was the best player on the freshman squad and getting better all the time. He liked every minute of practice and game time. It was only basketball that kept him in the big, new school that year.

During Jerry's sophomore year, his first season on the varsity, the West Virginia Mountaineers won 26 games and lost only 2. His team was picked by newspaper polls as the best college team in the country. And Jerry West was its star.

But being an athletic hero had drawbacks. Everybody at the school wanted to talk to him. Jerry was so shy that he blushed and stammered when he tried to reply. Even at the movies he often sat in the last row of the balcony so that he would not be seen.

As a junior, Jerry led West Virginia to the finals of the National Collegiate Athletic Association (NCAA) tournament. In the final game against California his team lost by a single point, but he was chosen the tournament's Most Valuable

Jerry pivots during fast action in a championship game between West Virginia and William and Mary in 1958.

Player, and was named to the All-American squad.

Gradually Jerry became more at ease with strangers. Still he remained a quiet, modest young man—except on the basketball floor. There he was known for daring, reckless play that won many games but also brought him many injuries.

In a game against Kentucky when he was a senior, Jerry broke his nose for the fourth time in college play. Bleeding and in pain, he had to be helped to the dressing room. After his nose had been bandaged and packed with ice, he came back to sit on the bench.

He watched worriedly as West Virginia fell behind. Finally he asked to go back in. At first the coach shook his head. But when Kentucky scored again, he waved Jerry back on the court. In the second half the plucky star scored 19 of the 33 points he made in the game. Once again Jerry West was named to the All-American basketball team.

After his graduation from West Virginia in 1960, Jerry was picked to play on the U.S. Olympic team in Italy. He and Oscar Robertson were made cocaptains to lead the finest U.S. basketball team in the history of the Olympic Games. Teams from fifteen foreign countries competed—among them Russia, Italy, Brazil, and Japan. The Americans swept through eight straight games to win gold medals.

When he returned from abroad, Jerry was the hero of his home state. He was so well known that the governor of West Virginia invited him to the state capitol.

When he reached the governor's office, a lady greeted him. "My name is Jerry West," he said politely. "I believe I have an appointment with the governor."

Jerry West and Oscar Robertson (center) were cocaptains of the gold-medal winning U.S. Olympic basketball team in 1960.

The lady smiled. "I know who you are, young man," she replied. "Why, you're better known than the governor himself."

Jerry had already decided to go into professional basketball. Each year the pro teams choose the college players they want to play for them. This is called the draft. The Los Angeles Lakers had picked Jerry West. Then they hired Fred Schaus, Jerry's former coach at West Virginia, to direct the team.

Jerry soon discovered that there is a big difference between college and professional basketball. The pro players were larger, more skillful, tougher, and more experienced.

Jerry West was a fine college shooter. He was quick and he was accurate, but he was only 6 feet, 3 inches tall. Among the pros he was a short man. He found it hard to play against the giant centers and forwards under the basket.

He saw that smaller men did better in the guard position, setting up plays in the backcourt and shooting from out on the court. So Jerry decided to learn all about backcourt play.

Jerry spent all the time he could trying to improve his ball handling and dribbling. He was always the first player out to practice and the last to leave. Before long Jerry had developed the skills he needed for the backcourt. At game time Jerry had the same drive and spirit he showed during practice. He was always ready to play, and play hard.

Once during his first season, Jerry came down with a bad cold. Although Jerry was ready to play, he expected to stay on the bench. Then he learned that the Lakers' star, Elgin Baylor, was too ill to put on a suit.

Without a word, Jerry stepped out to play the entire game. All the "sick" athlete did was score 38 points as the Lakers beat the Philadelphia Warriors, 126–116.

Los Angeles finished the season in second place. They lost the Western Division Play-Off to the St. Louis Hawks. But Jerry had a fine season.

However, a weakness from his college play still caused Jerry trouble. He could not move to his left as smoothly as to his right. Opposing teams began to force him to his left to keep him off balance. Jerry wanted to work on this problem.

The next summer he was a director at a boys' camp. This was the chance he needed. He would line up several twelve and thirteen-year-olds in front of him. Then he'd try to dribble through them, always moving to his left. He also worked on his jump shot.

Jerry's summer of practice and year of pro experience began to pay off in 1961–62. He had corrected his faults, and he had learned when to pass and when to shoot. His scoring average reached 30 points a game.

Elgin Baylor was the big star of the Los Angeles Lakers when Jerry joined them. Now these two men found they could work well together in the backcourt. They became a threat to other teams.

Jerry's outside jump shot made opposing coaches frantic. Two, and sometimes even three, defenders could not stop him. He would dribble to within twenty feet of the basket, and the ball would spin off his fingertips for another two points.

Jerry continued to play so hard that he was often injured. But he was seldom on the bench for long. Sportswriters, watching him in action, told each other, "The kid's good, all right. But he'll never last. He's too frail for this league." They often asked him if he didn't worry about his many injuries. "You can't worry about getting hurt and still do your job," he told them.

For all his shooting skill, Jerry West was an unselfish player. Once he scored 30 points in the first half of a game. A Laker teammate remembered the game with a smile.

"Jerry was really embarrassed at half

time," he said. "He was afraid we'd think he was hogging the ball."

West and Elgin Baylor led the Lakers to the Western Division title in 1961-62. Then they met the Boston Celtics for the national championship.

The Celtics had ruled pro basketball for several years, much as the New York Yankees once ruled the baseball world. Still West and Baylor thought the Lakers could take the title.

In the opener, K. C. Jones, the Celtics' brilliant guard, gave West a hard time. Jones clung to him closer than a shadow. Often he made Jerry hurry his shots, just enough to make them miss. Elgin Baylor scored 35 points, but Jerry did poorly. Boston outclassed the Western Division leaders easily in that first game. It looked as if they'd win the series in four straight games.

Jerry West did not sleep well that night. He was too angry—angry at himself. Losing was always a personal matter to Jerry. He made up his mind not to let it happen in the next game.

As the second game began, Jerry blasted off 11 points to put the Lakers ahead. The fast start upset the Celtics, and they were slow to catch up. By the third period the Lakers led 90–66.

All at once Boston began to click. The startled Lakers saw their big lead drop to 4 points. With six minutes left in the final quarter, the Celtics went ahead, 112–111.

Suddenly Jerry faked to his right, then to the left. A Boston guard leaped at him, but it was too late. The ball spun off Jerry's fingers. *Swish*. Two points—and the Lakers went on a rally of their own to win, 129–122.

The series was tied at one game apiece.

West and Bill Russell (left) go for a loose ball in the 1962 NBA Championship Finals. Below, West moves in on Celtics star Bob Cousy, who is attempting to dribble.

A record crowd jammed into the Los Angeles arena to watch the third contest. Both Jerry and Elgin were "hot" that night. They paced the Lakers to a 103–91 lead. But the Celtics fought back to go ahead 115–111 with only 58 seconds left.

Once more Jerry came to the rescue. He faked a pass and sent a long jump shot through the hoop. Then a Boston player fouled him, and he sank two free throws to tie the score at 115 all.

The Celtics took time out with exactly five seconds left in the game. They gathered near the sideline to set up the final play. Sam Jones, the Boston forward, took the ball for the throw-in.

Jerry West had a sudden "hunch" as he watched Jones. From the corner of his eye, he saw Bob Cousy's feet move a little. He darted in front of Cousy to steal Sam's pass. He dribbled the stolen ball a few strides, then banked it off the backboard. It zipped down through the net just as the buzzer sounded.

Final score: Lakers 117; Celtics 115.

Jerry was carried off the floor on the shoulders of his happy teammates. Although Elgin was high-point man with 39, it was Jerry's final great play that won the game.

The Celtics were stunned. Few players ever stole a basketball from Bob Cousy. His eyes downcast, Bob walked slowly off the court alone.

But the Lakers' triumph did not last. Boston captured the fourth, sixth, and seventh games to keep the title.

It was the 1969 Championship Play-Off between the Lakers and Boston that made the sports world realize that Jerry West was one of the greatest competitors in any sport. Although Wilt Chamberlain had now joined the Lakers, it was the hot shooting of Jerry West and Elgin Baylor that brought Los Angeles the Western Division title.

In the opening game against Boston, Jerry scored 53 points to lead the Lakers to a close 120–118 victory. He scored 41 points in the second contest to make it two in a row over the Celtics.

Finally the two teams reached the seventh and deciding game. The winner would be the NBA champion. With nine minutes left, the Lakers trailed, 100–83. Limping from an earlier injury, Jerry pulled himself together for a final effort.

The fans came to their feet as his jump shot swished through the basket. After that Jerry didn't stop until he had scored 14 points. It looked like the start of a winning rally. Then the Celtics came back strong to win by 2 points, 108–106.

Jerry shook his head sadly in the dressing room. After nine years in the NBA he still hadn't reached his goal—a national championship for the Lakers.

Each season as he fought toward that goal, Jerry gave his fans new thrills. One of them came in the 1972 All-Star game when Jerry was a member of the Western team.

Only nine seconds were left to play. The East and West were tied at 110 points apiece. The Westerners brought the ball inbounds after a time-out.

Now there were just two seconds left. Jerry dashed down the floor looking for a pass. Walt Frazier of the Eastern team was guarding him closely.

With one swift motion, Jerry pulled away from Frazier and caught the pass. His twenty-foot jump shot won the game for the Western team, 112–110. That helped him gain the Most Valuable Player award for the All-Star game.

But Jerry West and his Laker teammates had their eyes on the most important prize—the NBA championship. During the past dozen seasons the Lakers had reached the final play-off eight times. But in 1972 Los Angeles still waited for its first title.

That year they won the Western Division Play-Off by beating the Milwaukee Bucks in six games. Jerry played well on the court, but his shooting eye was off.

Late in the sixth game the Bucks had the lead. Then Jerry proved once more why he was nicknamed "Mr. Clutch." He took a pass from his backcourt partner, Gail Goodrich, and darted toward the basket. The ball sailed through the hoop. Before the final buzzer sounded he had scored 12 points.

Jerry West snatches a rebound away from the Knicks and gets into a scoring position in the 1972 NBA Championship Finals.

Now the Lakers faced the New York Knicks for the NBA championship. The Knicks won the first game, but from then on Jerry West and Wilt Chamberlain took charge. Jerry scored 21 points in the third game, but the fourth contest was his best.

The desperate Knicks, led by Bill Bradley's shooting, forced the Lakers into an extra period. With less than two minutes remaining in overtime play, Bradley tied the score once more with two baskets within 22 seconds. The scoreboard now read 111–111.

Twenty seconds later Jerry West coolly sank two free throws to put the Lakers ahead to stay. A field goal and a free throw by Gail Goodrich made the final score 116–111.

Then the Lakers won the fifth game. Los Angeles had its first NBA championship, and so did Jerry West. Cheering Laker fans swarmed out on the floor, and reporters questioned the players eagerly.

One newsman asked Jerry how he felt about his first championship. "I couldn't feel happier if we'd won ten titles," he said. It had taken Jerry West a long time to reach his goal, but his smile showed it was worth it.

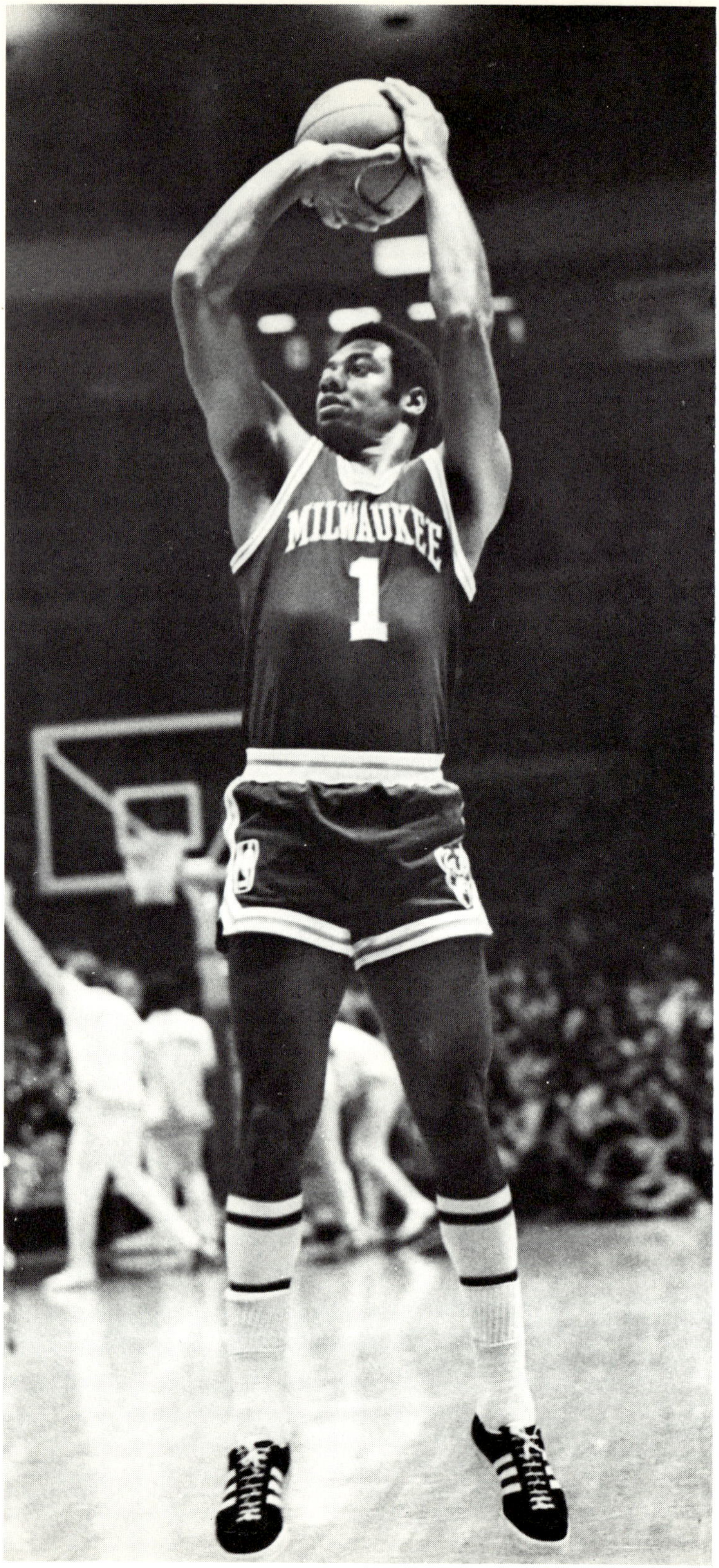
MILWAUKEE
1

Oscar Robertson
All-Around Player

When Oscar Robertson was a little boy, his mother bought him a small basketball. He liked it so much he took it everywhere he went. He'd dribble it along the sidewalk or twirl it on his fingers. He could spin it behind his back and catch it on the rebound. Before he went to bed at night, he even scrubbed the ball with soap and water.

"We always knew when Oscar was asleep," his mother said later. "That's when he stopped thumping the ball against the floor beside his bed."

"I had a feeling for a basketball even then," Oscar, the "Big O," recalled years later.

Oscar Palmer Robertson was born on November 24, 1938, at Charlotte, Tennessee, in a shack once owned by his grandfather.

When Oscar was a baby, the Robertson family moved to Indianapolis where his father worked for the city. But his parents soon separated, and his mother raised her three sons alone.

The boys grew up in the black ghetto. Money was scarce, and the boys had to make their own fun. Bailey, the oldest, became interested in basketball. He made a basket out of an old hoop and nailed it up behind the run-down little house. Some rags bound by rubber bands served as a ball.

Soon the two older brothers began to play at a nearby park playground. Little Oscar tagged along, but the bigger boys at the park chased him away.

"Run along, kid!" they'd all shout. "Go home and play with your rag ball."

Oscar would watch them with angry tears in his eyes. Then he would go home and shoot baskets by himself. This was the reason his mother bought him the little basketball.

One summer day he made his daily trip to the park to watch the older boys play. Not enough players showed up to form two full teams.

"Here, kid," one of them called to Oscar. "Get in until someone else shows up."

There was no stopping Oscar Robertson after that. Once he got his hands on a real ball, he made a place for himself in the daily playground game.

Soon everyone wanted him to play for them. "Hi, there," an older boy would shout as Oscar walked into the park. "You're on our side, man! Remember—you promised."

Oscar played basketball the year around. When he couldn't play outside, he played in the school gym or at the YMCA. As he became bigger and stronger, his skill grew.

His brother Bailey was the first of the family to make a name for himself on the court. Bailey became the star of the Crispus Attucks High School team in Indianapolis. His ball handling was so dazzling that he was asked to join the famous Harlem Globetrotters on an exhibition tour.

By the time Oscar entered Crispus Attucks High School, he was a better player than any boy on the freshman or varsity squads. He also proved to be a natural leader on the basketball floor. He quickly became the playmaker of his team, setting up the plays and giving the other players signals. Although he was the best shooter on the squad, he always fed his teammates passes. At the free-throw line he seldom missed.

Oscar led an all-black Crispus Attucks team to two straight state high school championships and a 45-game winning streak. He broke every Indiana high school record and was named to the all-state team three years in a row.

One of Oscar Robertson's happiest moments came when the team won its first state title. After the game the local fire department loaded the boys on a fire truck and paraded them through the city.

"We rode through the streets with the sirens wide open," said Oscar. "What a thrill! Then there was a bonfire and lots of cheering. It was inspiring—it really was."

By his senior year, Oscar had grown into a tall, handsome young man. He stood 6 feet, 2 inches tall, and he weighed 190 pounds. He was a fine all-around athlete, a winning baseball pitcher, and a high jumper in track.

Oscar was an excellent student too. He became a member of the National Honor Society and graduated in the upper tenth of his class.

When he finished high school, the young star received scholarship offers from colleges everywhere. No other high school athlete had more offers than he did.

Oscar chose the University of Cincinnati because it had one of the best teams in college basketball. But Oscar was interested in the courses the college offered, too. He took business subjects and had a part-time job in the office of the local gas and electric company.

Robertson scores a lay-up for Cincinnati in the famous Seton Hall game in 1958.

Oscar Robertson was the only black player on the Cincinnati basketball team. College rules kept him from playing varsity ball as a freshman, but he was the best of the first-year players.

As a sophomore, Oscar got his first big test when Cincinnati played a good Seton Hall team in Madison Square Garden in New York City.

New York fans knew their basketball. They were anxious to see the young player they had heard so much about. The crowd was buzzing with excitement when the two teams came on the floor. Was this serious-looking boy from the Middle West as good as people said he was?

The fans soon found out. They were startled to see Oscar race down the court and shoot the Cincinnati Bearcats into an early lead. The Big O was all over the floor.

Deep in his backcourt he would raise his arm, then shout, "Come on—on your toes—let's go!"

Then he'd dribble swiftly along the floor and fire a bullet pass to a forward. Sometimes he'd pass in to the pivot man, then spring beneath the basket to take a return toss and sink it for two points.

On defense he'd sing out, "Back—back—

drop back! I'll take the inside man! Hustle back there, gang!"

"Look at that kid control the ball," the fans shouted to each other. "Watch him set up plays."

"Yeah—and that defense!" the others called out. "He's all over the backboard."

A sportswriter, watching the game, spoke to his neighbor. "Robertson could play for the Knicks right now," he said. "Give him a little more experience, and he'll have a great future in pro ball."

The crowd forgot all about Seton Hall and the rest of the Bearcats as well. They stood and cheered as Oscar poured 56 points through the basket to set a new college scoring record for a single game. Oscar alone had scored 2 more points than the entire Seton Hall team.

After the game, the reporters quickly looked through the record book. "Hey,"

This basket on February 6, 1960, made Oscar the all-time major-college scoring king. The record held for a decade.

shouted one of them. "Another record. No high school, college, or pro player ever scored that many points in the Garden before!"

It was one of the finest sophomore performances in the history of college basketball. The Big O would hear those thundering cheers many times in the seasons ahead. While he was at Cincinnati, he became a three-time All-American player. During those seasons he led college scoring, and he set fourteen records before he graduated.

Oscar's teammates respected him so much that they never became jealous of his fame and honors. Once he appeared on a television program in New York. Back in Cincinnati a group of his teammates sat around a TV set watching.

"It's great to be an All-American player," said Oscar, "but my teammates deserve as much credit as I do. I couldn't have done it without them."

One of the players watching the program leaped to his feet. "The heck you couldn't, Big O," he shouted at the TV screen. "You're the greatest!"

Although Oscar was well liked by his teammates and fellow students, he faced problems that made him bitter at times. Sometimes—especially in the Deep South— he became angry and discouraged when he was not allowed to stay with the team in certain hotels because he was black. But this unfair treatment did not keep him from doing his best on the courts.

Oscar graduated from college in 1960 with a degree in business administration. That was the year of the Olympic Games at Rome, and he was chosen to play on the U.S. basketball team along with several other college stars. Among these was Jerry

West. Oscar and Jerry were named co-captains of the American squad.

When Oscar decided to turn pro, the Cincinnati Royals chose him in the college-player draft. The Royals had been near the bottom of the NBA standings for several seasons, and not many people came to their games. The Big O was very popular in the area so the owners knew the fans would come to see him in action.

The Big O now stood 6 feet, 5 inches tall, and he weighed a solid 215 pounds. He was fast, a fine shooter, and he could pass, dribble, or play defense. Besides he could jump high enough to match such heroes as Wilt Chamberlain.

Naturally everyone wanted to see how he would do playing against other stars in the professional league.

Although he had been a fine college player, Oscar did not become a pro star all at once. When he joined the Royals he was not sure of himself, and he had to learn their style of play.

But the Big O learned quickly. Soon he corrected his mistakes, and the other Royals began to accept him. They learned that if they found a way to get into the open, he'd find a way to pass to them. He began to show his skill as a playmaker again.

The rookie guard had an amazing first season. His scoring average rose steadily to 30 points a game. Only Wilt Chamberlain and Elgin Baylor did better than that. He was chosen to play on the 1960–61 NBA All-Star team, a rare honor for a first-year player.

By 1961–62, the other teams began to "double-team" Oscar: two opposing players guarded him all the time.

Actually this helped him. He learned to

The Big O struggles for a shot at the basket as Bill Russell guards him in a 1961 game with the Celtics.

fake one of his opponents out of position, and then flip the ball to an open teammate. Even better, this close guarding often caused him to be fouled. When he took a free throw after the foul, he almost never missed.

The Big O worked on his free-throw shooting all the time. Once the Royals' coach offered a prize to the player who could score the most free throws out of 25 shots. Three players tied at 23 apiece. Then Oscar stepped to the line. He scored all 25 attempts without a miss. He was proud of his skill at the free-throw line.

When Jerry Lucas joined the Royals, a writer asked the ex-Ohio State star what he thought of Oscar.

"I'm sure Robertson could boost his scoring record out of sight if he wanted to," replied Jerry. "But he's a team player through and through. Besides scoring, he gets us a dozen rebounds a game and ten or twelve assists. What more can you ask?"

The Big O usually gave the Boston Celtics a hard time. He always seemed at his best against them. For a while they tried to double, and even triple, team him. But nothing seemed to work.

Boston sometimes sent in three different guards against Oscar. They took turns trying to wear him down. One night speedy Sam Jones took the first shift. When he went to the bench panting at the end of the quarter, K. C. Jones, the Celtics' top defensive player took over. But the Big O kept right on scoring. Rugged John Havlicek came on next for Boston.

"Any signs of his slowing up yet?" asked John hopefully as he passed Jones at the sideline.

"That guy!" snorted K. C. "Are you kidding me?"

After the game, Red Auerbach, the Boston coach, chuckled. "We held Oscar tonight, all right. He only got 37 points."

Bill Russell, who coached the Celtics later, once said, "We let our guards argue among themselves about who covers Oscar. The one that loses gets the job."

Opposing teams learned it was a mistake to make the Big O angry. A guard from

Robertson dribbles past Willis Reed in a tough 1970 game.

another team once bumped Oscar off balance and blocked his shot. Robertson looked surprised when the referee did not call a foul.

When the same thing happened again, Oscar did not even glance toward the official. He took the ball at midcourt and moved forward slowly, pounding the ball against the floor as if daring anyone to stop him.

Suddenly he leaped and whipped the ball through the basket. He scored point after point before he began to set up plays again.

Everyone talked about Oscar Robertson's great shooting and playmaking ability. They sometimes overlooked his work on defense. When he was told to stop a high-scoring star, he usually did just that.

One player who found out about this the hard way was Bill Bradley, the brilliant

Princeton All-American forward. When Bradley joined the Knicks in 1967, he was already a deadly shooter. The first time he played against the Cincinnati Royals, Oscar was assigned to guard him.

Bill had never been really stopped in college. But now he was facing a man with several years of NBA experience behind him.

Bradley grabbed the ball after the tip-off and dribbled swiftly down the floor. As he set himself to shoot, a hand reached out and stole the ball. He whirled around to see the Big O already moving upcourt to set up a Cincinnati play.

The game quickly became a nightmare for Bill. He twisted and turned. He tried to shoot over Robertson. But each time he found a waving hand in his face.

The Big O allowed Bradley exactly two shots in the game, both of which he missed. Bill went on to become an NBA star, but he never forgot that first meeting with Oscar Robertson.

Wilt Chamberlain, who played against Oscar many times, once said, "There are faster men than the Big O, and some who can shoot better. But no one can beat him as an all-around player."

Oscar was voted the NBA's Most Valuable Player in 1964 by all the other players in the league. Although he stood 6 feet, 5 inches tall, he was the second smallest man ever to be so honored among the NBA giants. Bob Cousy of the Celtics, chosen in 1957, had been the smallest.

The Big O always plays hard, but he is a good sportsman. He seldom commits fouls himself and is respected for his clean play.

Once when the Royals met Detroit, the Detroit team had so many injuries that their lineup had to be changed around. A

Kareem Abdul-Jabbar (33) stands by as the Big O scores in a 1971 game between the Bucks and the Braves.

forward named Jackie Moreland was moved to the backcourt. He was to guard Robertson. To make matters worse, he had to play with a bandaged leg.

"Oscar quickly saw that I was limping," Moreland later recalled. "He could easily have driven through me toward the basket. I couldn't have stayed with him. Instead, he passed off to other players. He didn't want to take advantage of an injured player. I've always respected him for that."

Oscar Robertson remained at Cincinnati for ten years. He set scoring, assist, and rebound records. But the prize he wanted most of all passed him by. He wanted to win an NBA championship, and that never happened while he was with the Royals.

All this changed when he was traded to the Milwaukee Bucks, a new team in the league. The Bucks were led by 7-foot, 2-inch Kareem Abdul-Jabbar, who had brought them close to the NBA title the year before. But Jabbar needed more help. Someone had to be there to set up plays and run the team on the court. Milwaukee thought Oscar Robertson could do the job, and he joined the Bucks in the 1970–71 season.

With the Big O in their lineup, the Milwaukee team found what it needed most. Oscar called the plays and saw to it that Jabbar got the ball. When the huge center moved toward the basket, Oscar or a teammate would be ready to fire a bullet pass into his hands. Jabbar would swing around for a hook shot. *Swish*. Two more points for Milwaukee.

During the regular season the Bucks won 66 games and lost only 16. Then they won the Western Division Play-Off by defeating Los Angeles 4 games to 1. That placed them in the NBA championship

Robertson grabs a rebound (right) in the first game of the Championship Finals in 1972. He moves in for a basket (below) in the fifth game.

finals against the Baltimore Bullets, the Eastern champions.

The Bullets were no match for Milwaukee as the Bucks won in four straight games. Newsmen called the last game one of the best of Oscar's career. By scoring 30 points and setting up shots for Jabbar, Oscar spearheaded the Bucks to a final victory of 118-106.

Like Wilt Chamberlain and Jerry West, the Big O had finally reached his greatest basketball goal, one that meant more to him than all the records and personal honors that came his way—at last he, Oscar Robertson, was a member of an NBA championship team.